GIFT OF TEARS

Gift of Tears is intended for people who find that they have to cope, in the course of their work or their daily lives, with the grief of others. They may be teachers, nurses, policemen and women, doctors, personnel officers, for example, or just neighbours and friends.

The anguish of another – whether for a lost pet or the consequences of a brutally sudden bereavement – touches on the whole personality of the individual called upon to help. The main aim of this book is to help carers to contemplate and then to confront their own relationship to loss, the better to cope with the loss of others. The authors, who have run many training courses for such varied professions as nursing, probation work, medicine, social work, teaching and the clergy, present loss as a natural event which people can be helped to understand and work through.

Using a unique mixture of theory and counselling practice, Susan Lendrum and Gabrielle Syme bring the practice alive through accessible case-histories and also through exercises which invite the reader to become more involved. They look at the variable circumstances in which losses occur for both adults and children, and discuss historical and cultural variations in attitudes to loss, grieving and death. Particularly helpful to those training to work with loss is a section on developing professional skills, supervision and training, followed by a list of the resources available for carers.

Susan Lendrum and **Gabrielle Syme** work as psychotherapists, counsellors, supervisors, trainers and consultants to psychotherapy and counselling courses.

GIFT OF TEARS

A Practical Approach to Loss and Bereavement Counselling

Susan Lendrum
and
Gabrielle Syme

London and New York

First published in 1992
by Routledge
11 New Fetter Lane, London EC4P 4EE

Simultaneously published in the USA and Canada
by Routledge
29 West 35th Street, New York, NY 10001

Reprinted 1992 and 1993

© 1992 Susan Lendrum and Gabrielle Syme

Typeset in Palatino by Michael Mepham, Frome, Somerset
Printed and bound in Great Britain by
Mackays of Chatham PLC, Chatham, Kent.

A Tavistock/Routledge publication

British Library Cataloguing in Publication Data
A catalogue record for this book is available from the British
Library.

Library of Congress Cataloging in Publication Data
Lendrum, Susan, 1942–
Gift of tears: a practical approach to loss and bereavement
counselling / Susan Lendrum and Gabrielle Syme.
p. cm.
Includes bibliographical references and index.
1. Loss (Psychology) 2. Bereavement—Psychological
aspects. 3. Death—Psychological aspects. I.Syme,
Gabrielle, 1943– II. Title.
BF575.D35L46 1992
155.9′37—dc20
91–43922
CIP

ISBN 0–415–08120–3
0–415–07349–9 (pbk)

This book is dedicated to David, Robert and all our children

Before the beginning of years
There came to the making of man
Time with a gift of tears,
Grief with a glass that ran.
A.C. Swinburne, *Atalanta in Calydon*

CONTENTS

CONTENTS

Section IV Complicated grief

Section V Professional implications

Appendices

EXERCISES

TABLES

ACKNOWLEDGEMENTS

We wish to acknowledge the many clients, students and others whose losses have touched our lives and from whom we have learned so much. Our children in particular have taught us, often with great patience, how to respond more usefully to the losses in their lives.

Brenda Wood has quietly typed away in the background, supplying comfort and coffee in appropriate quantities.

INTRODUCTION

Many of those who work with people in a helping capacity or just as fellow humans come across loss in the course of these human interactions. For instance, we might notice tears in a friend's eyes as we chat over coffee about last night's television programme. In a more formal context, as a teacher for example, we might be puzzled by the behaviour of a child whose parents are divorcing; or as a social worker, be troubled by an elderly person's difficulties when faced with residential care; or as a doctor, feel anger when a patient talks of his redundancy notice; or as a nurse, feel anxious when talking to relatives of a dying patient; or as a father, feel helpless when a daughter cannot be reconciled to the loss of a pet; or we may be just confused when a neighbour cannot seem to get over her youngest leaving home. Of course, we may also have been, indeed we may also still be, or may soon be, that awkward child, that lonely old person, that redundant worker, that bereaved relative, that abandoned parent. There is a sense in which all of us have suffered and share in the suffering of every kind of loss.

When the two of us sat down to write this book we remembered how we had met, one of us a physiologist and the other a linguist, and had talked to one another of the very different losses we had each experienced. We remembered how frightened and alone we had each felt with our separate griefs and how often we had hidden our tears from other people. By the time we met we had each been enabled, through the presence of another person, to work through our separate griefs and to lay down some of the burdens we had been carrying. We had also worked, in different contexts, with many who had suffered loss. We decided to set up courses together to train those who were working with the grieving. We were aware of the fear of grief in society and yet we also knew, with Swinburne, that grief is an integral part of the time-span of human life and that tears are the natural response.

In thinking about the elements that had helped reduce our own fears, we realised what we valued in particular. At an emotional level, we remembered the invaluable presence of another in our grief work, and at a cognitive level, the knowledge we had received from training. Knowledge gained from studies of adult and child bereavement and from studies on the effectiveness of different helping responses; knowledge about depression and about the responses to loss of people from other cultures and ideas from both the humanistic and the more psychodynamic tradition have all thrown light for us on how to BE with a person who has suffered a loss.

In this book we attempt to share what we have learned, emotionally and cognitively, from these different sources. By condensing what has been a necessarily long and drawn-out process we may well make it all seem simpler than it is. The mistakes we have made with clients, trainees, colleagues and friends were no doubt as important as our other sources of learning. But we hope that, even in the simplified form of this book, our experience can be of some use to the man or woman faced by another's grief and wondering: 'What on earth do I say now?', 'How can I handle these tears?', 'Why do I feel scared?', 'Why am I angry?'.

Anyone working with someone who is grieving will experience strong feelings themselves. Indeed we hope this book will evoke feelings in you, as well as thoughts and ideas. As we discovered for ourselves, such strong feelings can sometimes be overwhelming unless they are spoken in the presence of someone who will accept – and not judge. For this reason we would strongly encourage you to use this book not on your own, but with others, in a group as part of a training programme, or in counselling supervision, or with a trusted colleague or friend.

Strong feelings are part of the natural response to loss, and tears their human expression. We know the value of tears in releasing and expressing feelings, and we know that counsellors need to learn to feel comfortable with tears. This ease with tears is acquired in part through an understanding and acceptance of our own and others' tears and associated feelings; in part through learning how to respond to feelings in others; and in part through the use of professional help in working with those who have suffered loss. Our relative ease with tears has been made possible through the many men and women who have taught us and shared their lives with us.

Counsellors and the counselled can be male or female. We have therefore sometimes used 'he' and at other times 'she'. If the counsellor is female, we have usually made the counselled male. In all such cases, the 'he' can be read as 'she' and vice versa. However, there are some cases where it is important for counsellor and counselled to be of the same sex; an example is the story of Vilna in chapter 13. When referring to children in general, rather than to a particular child, we have used 'she' throughout.

We have deliberately avoided the word 'client' in the early chapters, as we are aware that many people who use counselling skills, when listening to someone's sorrow and grief, would not necessarily see themselves as offering counselling to a client. However, later in the book, particularly from chapter 9 on, where we use exercises and vignettes to illustrate the points we are making, we have for clarity used the words client and counsellor. Some other words used commonly in our language take on different and perhaps deeper meanings in this book, for instance 'feeling-less-ness' and 'way-of-being'. Their meanings should emerge from their contexts.

All the characters and stories recounted in this book are fictitious and truthful at the same time. They have been drawn from our experience (in life and as practising counsellors), but transformed and combined so as to detach them entirely from any possible resemblance to people we know. If you think you have met one of our characters then you will have discovered that life is no less painful than fiction and that human loss is universal.

Section I

LOSS AND NURTURE

1

EARLY ATTACHMENTS AND LOSS

NATURAL OR NECESSARY LOSSES

To be born, a baby must leave the womb; to grow up and leave its mother, a baby needs to be weaned. The child entering school and learning about the world needs to leave its parents, and then adolescents have the task of leaving their own family in order to set up their own separate lives. These 'leavings' constitute much of the loss which human beings in our culture experience as part of the natural process of growing up and eventually of death.

In thinking of these stages only as development or 'growing up' it is easy to forget the place of loss in growth and change. These losses, which happen to the majority of us, could be called 'necessary losses' (Viorst, 1989) and they usually evoke strong feelings. As babies, such feelings find powerful and direct expression. Think of the baby sleeping who awakens and lies quietly for a bit, but suddenly starts to cry lustily, as if it cannot bear to be alone any more. The cry is usually very compelling to the mother and appears to demand a response and a re-establishment of human connection. The younger the baby is, the shorter the time it can bear on its own. Weaning a baby is not just a nutritional process but also an emotional process in which the infant gradually manages longer periods on its own; with maturity comes the capacity to be alone. People who study babies propose that this is because babies gradually develop the knowledge that their parent will return and that the loss or absence is survivable meanwhile (Stern, 1985). In other words, as we mature we discover inner resources and knowledge. Without increasing periods alone and the consequent experience of loss we would not mature. These losses are termed necessary losses.

Each one of these necessary losses resulting from separation needs to be comforted. Given enough comfort, each loss successfully managed is a step towards independence and growing self-awareness. We do not necessarily remember these losses but we are shaped by them, for they become part of our inner emotional world. We have learnt that loss is survivable, and as we begin to face loss more consciously we can discover inner resources.

Exercise 1.1 Lost child

It is 4 p.m. on a wintry afternoon. Tom (2) and his mother, Mary, are in the shopping centre. Mary is tired and keen to get home. She thinks Tom is still in tow. Tom, however, has been distracted by some moving toy he's just spotted. After a minute or two he turns to tell her and realises she's not there. As he realises she's not there, he emits a piercing and penetrating scream which seems to blot out all other sounds.

Imagine how Tom would feel and continue the story.

Mothers 'know' about and draw on these resources in their handling of their babies and children, responding intuitively with the comfort they need.

SHORT SEPARATIONS

To focus on your own 'intuitive' knowledge of loss, consider the example in Exercise 1.1 of a child lost and separated from his mother in a crowded shopping centre.

If you were able to get inside Tom's skin you will have noticed some strong feelings. These probably included shock, disbelief, terror, fear and anger. Your ability to recall these feelings draws on your memory and your understanding that others feel similar things in similar situations.

You also know that Tom's mother's experience of the same event will be different. This is told in Exercise 1.2.

Exercise 1.2 Mother's response

As Mary suddenly realises that Tom's not there, her heart misses a beat. She hears the piercing scream and tries to rush towards him, but the centre is crowded and her way is barred. Despite her tiredness she finds sudden energy to get through the crowd and reaches Tom within a few seconds. She shouts and rages at him for a minute. As she gradually calms down, she realises he is frightened too. She puts her arms round him, cuddles him, calms him down and sets off home. When they get home they tell the family all about their frightening afternoon.

Imagine and list the various feelings Mary experienced.

In thinking about Mary's feelings you will have recognised fear, anger, frustration and relief. You can respond to the story because you know intuitively how people are likely to feel in a frightening situation. Tom's frightened, angry cry was his way of trying to get his mother back. Mary's anger fuelled her drive to get through the crowd. Anger is one of the very strong feelings that arises when we fear a loss. Even when she found Tom again it took time for her fear and anger to subside.

Fortunately the loss was brief and her fear manageable so she was able quickly to comfort him in the way he needed. They each told the tale when they got home which helped them to deal with the experience. In the words of Shakespeare in *Macbeth*, it is not only 'sorrow' but fear and anger which need to be 'given words' when a loss has occurred (see page 187).

The powerful feelings of shock, fear, terror, anger and frustration evoked in Tom and Mary through even this very brief separation are not surprising. Research into the power of human attachment and especially the bonding of young children to their attachment figures or carers, most frequently their mothers, confirms that such unforeseen separations are very frightening for good reasons.

SOME STUDIES OF ATTACHMENT BEHAVIOUR

Sigmund Freud, who recognised the enormous influence of childhood experiences on adult emotional life, wrote about the strength of early attachments. He recognised this most basic of all human drives towards forming and sustaining attachments to others, yet seemed to understand it purely as a feeding relationship; primarily as cupboard love. Of course for the new-born baby the balance between life and death hangs upon the success of this relationship and the attendant ability to deal with hunger, pain and illness. But is this all there is to the mother and baby relationship?

John Bowlby, a psychoanalyst interested in childhood development, thought not. He was interested in more recent studies made by biologists such as Konrad Lorenz and Nicolaas Tinbergen, who observed patterns of behaviour in birds and other animals. They noticed that many species of bird forged strong and specific attachment bonds. Lorenz's goslings 'locked' on to the first moving object in sight (most usually the mother goose, but occasionally Lorenz himself!); while many of Tinbergen's birds, having 'locked' on to a bird of the opposite sex, had remained mates throughout life (Bowlby, 1969).

The new-born baby does not, of course, 'lock' on to the first moving object and will be relatively undiscriminating about the person who attends to its needs in the early months. At this stage the baby is thought to be unaware of itself as a separate person. By about 6 months, however, a very marked preference for one person develops. It is as though the baby, having recognised its separateness and aloneness, 'decides' to counter this terrible aloneness by falling in love with the very person recognised as 'other' and yet who is also familiar. Anyone judged 'unfamiliar' is likely to be firmly rejected at this stage. As women suckle babies and in our culture generally also tend to their physical needs and interact with them in the process, mothers are usually, but not necessarily, the chosen attachment figures. It appears that the need for human connection is fundamental. 'The love of others comes into being simultaneously with the recognition of their existence', wrote Ian Suttie in 1935. As soon as we can distinguish 'you' and 'me' we seem almost to fall in love, perhaps to try to assuage the terror and isolation of that very separateness.

Experiments by Harry Harlow (1961), using a range of wire model 'monkey-mothers', showed that baby rhesus monkeys would thrive best and form attachments only to wire substitutes which were covered in cloth and gave 'contact comfort' – in other words were 'cuddly'. In other experiments where the infant monkeys were alarmed or in a strange setting, only those with cloth models were comforted sufficiently to start to explore. It looks, therefore, as though monkeys are 'programmed' to stay close to a cuddly mother, thus finding protection from predators which might harm them. Only with this security are they able to explore, play and mature. This attachment behaviour is found in the young of most species of mammals and birds. Its likely function is self-preservation, in that an immature animal seeks close proximity to an adult who in turn will protect it from danger.

Baby humans seem also to be 'programmed' to stay close to mother to find protection from danger. Babies who did not have a mother or mother-figure to stay close to and who were hospitalised from birth were studied by René Spitz in America in the early 1940s. He found that babies whose hunger, pain and illness needs had been methodically attended to, but who had 'only 1/8th of a nurse', were severely retarded developmentally, both mentally and physically (Spitz, 1945). It would seem that a reliable early attachment is of vital importance to healthy development and the cost of breaking that bond, as in institutional care with a low carer to baby ratio or with 'wire mothers', may be very high.

Quality of attachment

Attachment behaviour was observed in more detail by a team led by Mary Ainsworth (1978), one of Bowlby's co-workers. In observing the reactions of infants who had been left alone for 3 minutes in a standardised strange situation and were then reunited with their mothers, she found three distinct patterns of response. The majority of babies were upset during the separation episode and explored little. On their mother's return they would respond strongly, seeking close bodily contact, and insist on interacting with her. A second group of babies showed no distress during separation and on reunion avoided contact and interaction with their mother. The smallest group of all were anxious, even before separation, and were enormously upset during the separation, but on reunion, although they wanted close contact, they resisted interaction. Ainsworth described the first group of children as 'securely attached' and observed that the mothers of these children were sensitive and positively responsive to them. The other two groups were said to be 'anxiously attached' and either 'avoidant' or 'ambivalent'. The avoidant children had mothers who were rejecting and with an aversion to physical contact. These mothers were frequently angry but showed little facial expression. The ambivalent children's mothers were not rejecting, seemed to enjoy physical contact but were singularly insensitive. Ainsworth and her team concluded that attachment behaviour and response to separation is markedly affected by the mother's personality.

Secure attachment: short separation

Let us return now to Mary and her son Tom, and let us assume that Mary and Tom had been able to form a secure attachment. As Tom had developed within this basically secure relationship there had always been someone there for him to turn to in threatening situations. As he had begun to crawl and then walk his movement was always 'away', moving towards independence and discovery of the world. All this was possible within the secure knowledge of Mary's presence, with the occasional backward glance for reassurance. Gradually the 'secure base' which Mary offered out there began to be assimilated and to develop within Tom so that she did not always have to be in sight. He could tolerate her absence and could re-connect to her when she returned. When he did lose her in the shopping centre he emitted a scream so powerful, and full of 'hope-of-retrieving-her', that Mary was quickly with him and the period of loss brief. She was able to comfort him, he felt secure again and the loss was managed.

This early secure attachment of Tom's provides inner resources which will help him to manage later in stressful and even threatening situations. However, if the attachment is anxious then it is more difficult to explore and to cope with separation. Thus the capacity of infants to manage a threatening and stressful situation, such as the loss of an attachment figure, will depend on the quality of the early attachments. Additional factors which affect this capacity are the duration of the loss, the frequency of losses with little recovery time, the maturity of the child and the presence, warmth and caring capacity of other familiar figures.

Secure attachment: longer separation

To illustrate the effect of a longer separation on a securely attached child let us return to Tom and his mother in Exercise 1.3. In this instance the separation could be described as traumatic or circumstantial rather than natural.

Exercise 1.3 Child in hospital

Unfortunately, a few months later Tom fell off the slide and bumped his head so badly that he was dazed for some minutes. When he was violently sick some time later, Mary decided to take him to casualty. They kept him in hospital for observation. She was able to stay with him. When Tom nodded off, she took the chance to go and telephone her husband to tell him where they were. There was a long queue for the telephone, and Mary had to wait for about 20 minutes to complete her call.

Meanwhile Tom had woken up and realising that his mother was missing, he screamed. When she did not reappear, he started rushing frantically all over the ward. Nobody could comfort or calm him. The nurses were beginning to feel frantic. Then he suddenly went quiet, which was a relief for the nurses. However, the peace was short-lived and Tom soon repeated his frantic searching, to be followed again by a quiet and withdrawn period.

When Mary returned, his withdrawal shocked her. He initially 'ignored her' and she had to coax him into letting her cuddle him.

Now try to identify the different feelings that Tom experienced.

The further feelings you may have thought about may be frustration and panic; you may even have wondered about hopelessness and despair. In this story Tom's angry cry did not bring his mother back, so he started rushing frantically around as though he were searching for her. He still thought he would find her and felt hopeful. Yet his mother's longer absence

Table 1.1 Summary of an experience of a sudden longer loss for a child

Child's feeling	Child's state of belief	Child's behaviour
MOTHER GOES AWAY		
Shock and anger	Disbelief that mother has gone.	Scream to recover mother.
Angry longing	Disbelief that mother has really gone.She can still be found.	Rushing around searching; crying.
Despair and hopelessness	Belief that mother has gone.	Withdrawal.
Emptiness	She cannot be found.	Silence. (Short-term denial of needs and feelings.)
MOTHER RETURNS		
Scared	Dare I believe what I see.	Watching and waiting. Lets self be hugged but does not respond.
Fear wanes	I'll risk believing.	Begins to respond.
Relief	I can believe. I dare relate.	Reattached.

this time had raised his fear and panic to such an extent that he had almost given up hope and begun to feel despair. This made it more difficult for her to soothe and reassure him. Tom's experience of loss is summarised in Table 1.1.

Tom's response to the longer separation is typical of the responses found by James and Joyce Robertson when they made some very poignant films in the 1950s documenting the reactions of children separated from their parents on admission to hospital or a residential nursery. All the children over the age of 6 months were found to respond to the separation in predictable ways. Initially they would protest loudly, search frantically and show acute distress. To an onlooker it was clear that the children were moving heaven and earth to retrieve their lost mothers. This phase was then followed by despair in which they became inactive and withdrawn, though they might well repeat the word 'Mummy' monotonously. Children would frequently return to protesting and then back into despair more than once before the third stage was reached.

In this final stage the children became detached, apparently not noticing when an individual nurse came and went. The longer the stay in hospital or nursery the worse the situation became. Although children would try to form an attachment to a nurse, for instance, she would then leave to go off duty. The more often these transient mother-figures were lost the more detached these children became, eventually ceasing to show any feelings or any care for anyone.

Later research, in work by Bowlby and others, has shown that the quality of a child's early attachment will influence both the persistence with which she tries to form new attachments, and the quality and persistence of her detachment. Where the early attachments are reasonably secure the child will persist for longer in trying to make attachments and may make a lot of fuss about each departure. She will, however, be less damaged by each departure. Where the early attachments are less secure and more anxious each departure may be so painful that the child seems to separate herself from her feelings and makes little fuss when people depart. On the surface she appears quite quiet and settled and much less trouble to the staff than the securely attached child. But underneath she may be denying the very feelings and experiences which, however uncomfortable at the time, are part of the natural grieving process.

These differences are also apparent when the mother returns. Even for the securely attached child, it will be difficult. She will probably ignore her mother initially and need considerable coaxing to relate to her again. For the insecurely attached child, it may be impossible for her to risk a relationship again and she remains detached, cut off from her mother and denying her true feelings. This could be understood as a logical conclusion to all she has experienced and seems to ensure that she is not hurt again.

These observations have eventually had profound effects on hospital policy so that it is now commonplace for hospitals to enable parents to stay with their ill children, just as Mary stayed with Tom.

In Tom's case he was deprived of Mary for so long that he was overwhelmed with despair and at first needed to deny his relationship. Fortunately, he was attached securely enough to Mary to have the capacity to bear the anxiety of separation and the angry feelings he experienced towards her. It took Mary time to comfort him and patience to remember that his angry feelings were entirely appropriate to his situation. In spite of the more severe difficulties associated with this loss Tom was none the less able to reattach and 'manage' the loss. For others the experience of loss is not managed by reattachment but by continued denial of feelings and withdrawal from relationships.

ORIGINS OF DENIAL

Where the early attachments are very anxious and insecure, the number of losses too frequent, the duration too long or the capacity of the attachment figures to offer comfort and support very low, then the direct expression of feelings and needs becomes increasingly difficult and instead the true feelings are denied. This denial of the existence of feelings is a way of separating and thus 'protecting' ourselves from too frightening or too painful feelings. In this way we can come to convince ourselves that we are unaffected by the loss and in turn convince others of this make-believe. When this happens grief may seem to disappear, but signs of locked-in feelings such as coldness and uninvolvement signal that grief has 'gone underground' or become blocked. A relationship of trust is required to free this block so that the denied feelings of childhood can find expression. A skilled and experienced helper will be able to facilitate the expression of these locked-in feelings.

EARLY SEPARATIONS AND ADULT LOSS

Linking the Robertsons' observations of a pattern of response to a longer loss with Ainsworth's observations of types of attachment, it is possible to see how children will respond to separation with a predictable pattern of feelings, and how this pattern will be affected by the quality of the early relationship. It also becomes clear that adult responses to loss will be as varied as this early experience.

At one end of the spectrum where children have been securely attached, then in both later childhood and in adult life they will be able to trust others to understand, validate and comfort the strong feelings associated with separations and other kinds of loss, and will be able to tolerate these for themselves. At the other end, where children have been insecurely attached, then they will be unable to trust others to validate their feelings and may react in a variety of ways. Some may deny the strong feelings, detach from the experience and appear untouched or even deadened. Others may seem to be stuck in one part of the pattern and express only one feeling in an exceptionally concentrated way which can seem bizarre to observers. Indeed this can be so extreme and intense that some people refer to these grief responses as 'abnormal', 'atypical', 'unnatural', 'morbid' or even 'pathological'. We have found it more useful to think of all these human responses to loss as lying along a spectrum of responses ranging from less to more complicated forms of a common fundamental pattern. Extreme behaviour patterns in adults may indicate a particularly complicated form of response to loss.

Of course most people's responses will be somewhere in between the two ends of the spectrum, with wide variation in terms of the kind of response, the intensity and duration of denial, the ability to trust themselves not to be overwhelmed by these feelings and the ability to trust others to validate and comfort them.

A knowledge of this spectrum of human responses and its relationship to attachment history is useful in working with the grieving. It enables helpers to understand more about individual difference and to focus appropriately. It can also enable them to assess early on whether a person might need a longer-term helping relationship which would focus on early separations and losses. This type of assessment is discussed in more detail in chapter 14.

SUMMARY

1 Loss and separation form an intrinsic part of human emotional development. These losses are therefore known as necessary losses.
2 Readers know from their own life experience the emotional responses of both a parent and a child when they are suddenly separated.
3 Attachment behaviour is genetically endowed and concerns the survival of young animals.
4 Studies on attachment behaviour in young children show that attachment can be secure or anxious and, within the latter category, can be ambivalent or avoidant.
5 The response of a securely attached child to a short natural separation and a longer unexpected separation can be predicted.
6 The response of an anxiously and insecurely attached child to a short natural separation or a longer unexpected separation can also be predicted and differs from that of a securely attached child in two major ways. These are that the child will remain detached and become cut off from her feelings. She will protect herself from too painful feelings by denying their existence.
7 The early attachment history and experiences of separation affect the adult response to loss. This results in a wide variety of responses to loss or bereavement.
8 The wide variety of responses lie on a spectrum with a common fundamental pattern.

2

THE NURTURING ENVIRONMENT
Aspects of the counselling approach

In the last chapter we pointed out how Tom's mother felt fearful and angry when she lost him, but was quickly able to accept her feelings. She could then nurture Tom by comforting and consoling him when she reached him. We also considered the role which feelings play in responses to loss, and their function in ensuring care and comfort in young humans and, indeed, in young mammals. The response to loss, of course, becomes more complex and differentiated as we grow and develop; but some very basic reactions

---

Exercise 2.1 Helpful and unhelpful responses

Go back into the past, near or distant, and think of a time in your life which was difficult for you. Try to remember the event itself, think about that time, ponder on what was happening then and see if you can recall how other people responded to you. You will remember things that were said as well as attitudes which you sensed. Try to categorise these into responses which were helpful or unhelpful.

HELPFUL RESPONSES   **UNHELPFUL RESPONSES**

---

remain with us all our lives and are part of our essential humanness. Accepting these reactions is part of our ability to comfort and console others. Mary had an accepting attitude to her own feelings. She trusted, accepted and listened to them, perhaps intuitively, and thus was sensitive to Tom's needs. Her ability to do this depended to a large extent on her own experience of secure attachments. As she was nurtured so was she able to nurture.

Counselling is a way of helping people to trust, accept and listen to themselves and their feelings. It is characterised by a set of attitudes, towards both self and others, which aims to foster trust and self-acceptance. These attitudes are often there when people are trying to help and comfort one another. Sometimes they are not around and we encounter unhelpful and even painful responses. Exercise 2.1 offers you the opportunity to use your own experience of life, to find the range of attitudes you met when you needed help and comfort.

A major aim of this book is to use your own experience as an integral part of learning about loss counselling. It is useful in this context to think about the event which you chose and consider the ways in which loss was a part of the event, or indeed the core of the event.

You may find yourself feeling quite angry now as you remember these unhelpful responses. Generally the unhelpful responses are linked with the listener being non-accepting, having judgemental attitudes, being a poor listener and perhaps themselves being overwhelmed by the story. This often leads to statements such as:

You'll get over it	Cheer up
Don't cry! Crying only upsets you	Give us a smile
Least said soonest mended	It was meant to happen
Every cloud has a silver lining	There's light at the end
It'll all come out in the wash	of the tunnel

and in the case of loss and bereavement statements such as:

Don't be morbid	You're better off without him/her
Never speak ill of the dead	It's time *you* got back to normal (6 weeks later!)
Of course you'll find someone else	It's God's will
There are more pebbles on the beach	It was meant

All these remarks make the person who is hurt feel devalued, angry and misunderstood. Although the listener may be trying consciously to respond to the person in distress, their unhelpful remarks may function on the surface to comfort the person making the remark and cover their embarrassment. Unconsciously they deny the listener's *own* fear of death and pain, and fill the potentially painful silence. They may also reflect society's difficulty in accepting death and the strong feelings which we have about dying.

Helpful responses, on the other hand, usually include a recognition of feelings, an understanding that the feelings being experienced may be frightening for that person, and that those who are frightened or lost may behave in odd ways. They will usually recognise that what is happening is unique for that individual. The person in trouble who receives helpful responses has the experience of receiving undivided attention, and does not feel they are a burden to the listener. These helpful responses lead to the person in difficulty feeling accepted and understood so that the experience of hurt and pain is truly recognised. This capacity to accept and not judge is the first of three basic attitudes which characterise the 'way-of-being' of a counsellor. A counsellor in training will not just learn about appropriate responses, but will also be encouraged to adopt and foster the basic attitudes underlying any responses. This first attitude is usually called 'acceptance'.

A second attitude is demonstrated when listeners are able to sense, very accurately, what is being felt and yet not be overwhelmed by those feelings. This is what counsellors call empathic understanding or 'empathy'. That is the capacity to feel with others and to enter the world of their feelings as if it were one's own without the distancing effects of either fear or pity. Fear makes it difficult for us really to hear the true experience of the other, and pity can become a barrier that puts down the other person. This is succinctly worded by Dea Trier Mørch (1982) when she says: 'You don't help another person with pity. You don't have to suffer too. You have to be what you are.'

The origins of empathic relating are in our earliest relationships. The capacity for empathy may be enhanced or diminished by subsequent relationships and experiences. Counsellor selectors are looking for this basic empathic capacity when they select counsellors for training. This capacity can be enhanced through training and supervision.

A third attitude called 'congruence', or sometimes genuineness, is less easily understood. We are in a state of congruence when we can be real and genuine and not make ourselves out to be what we are not. Our inner feelings are clear to us and are reflected in our behaviour. Congruent counsellors accept themselves as they are and convey this sense of self-acceptance to the other. This enables a more trusting and safer relationship to develop.

These attitudes are, of course, not exclusive to counsellors, but are those fostered in counselling training of all kinds. Truax and Carkhuff's (1967) seminal research on therapeutic relationships demonstrated that when these attitudes are present in the helping relationship then growth, change and healing take place. These findings have been replicated in various western countries. A summary of this way-of-being is in Table 2.1.

Table 2.1 Basic attitudes of counselling

Counselling is most effective when the counsellor can:
1 Offer complete and unconditional acceptance
2 Feel and communicate empathic understanding
3 Be congruent or genuine

One of the difficulties in writing about acceptance, empathy and congruence is that they are not as easy to demonstrate as they sound. There are times when they are particularly difficult to experience and demonstrate towards another person. Knowledge of ourselves enables us to recognise when our feelings are not congruent. If an incongruent feeling develops and persists so that it intrudes on the ability to listen, then it is worth reflecting on this and deciding where this feeling is coming from. A counsellor's response to loss in her own life may be sparked off by the experiences or feelings of the griever and then she may be responding to her own loss rather than the griever's loss. This is often what is happening when the counsellor is finding it particularly difficult to maintain the basic attitudes of acceptance, empathy and congruence. This in turn is one of the reasons why supervision from another individual is so important in counselling work; for without the maintenance of these basic attitudes counselling is ineffective. The form and function of supervision will be discussed in chapter 15.

Counselling developed out of Carl Rogers' convictions that the seeds of healing are to be found within each individual (Rogers, 1967). From the previous chapter we know that each person's response to loss is the unique product of their own individual experience. Counselling, with its emphasis on listening to the individual, is particularly suited to helping someone through the work of grieving a loss.

In section II we consider the experience of death and bereavement as a specific example of human loss, before moving on in section III to consider how counselling attitudes can foster a set of more helpful responses in practice.

SUMMARY

1 Certain attitudes towards feelings are more helpful than others in fostering growth and healing the wounds of grief.
2 Responses which demonstrate an accepting attitude are more helpful.
3 Three particular attitudes create the necessary conditions for change in a helping relationship. These are acceptance, empathy and congruence.
4 Research indicates that these attitudes are effective.

Section II

DEATH AS A PARTICULAR FORM OF LOSS

3

EXPERIENCES OF DEATH AND BEREAVEMENT

Within the course of any human life there are very many different experiences of loss. Some losses such as birth, weaning and death happen to all of us and can be called 'necessary losses' (see chapter 1). Because they all lead to separateness, and are an integral part of development and maturation, they are often also called 'developmental losses'. However, these are only some of the losses we may experience as part of the cycle of life and death.

CIRCUMSTANTIAL LOSSES

There are other losses which do not happen to all of us and which might not at first appear to lead to personal development. However, these circumstantial losses, as they are sometimes called, can themselves become sources of personal growth and maturity. Some of these losses are listed in Exercise 3.1 on the following page.

At a first glance some of these events are more obviously associated with loss than others. The less obvious ones may be fire, birth of a handicapped child, sexual abuse, rape, infertility and going into hospital. We have included these because whenever someone feels safe enough to ponder their experience of such an event, the word 'loss' or 'lost' comes in. In recalling, for instance, sexual abuse as a child, many people mention loss of innocence, loss of control, loss of trust, loss of self-esteem, loss of dreams, loss of ideals. In talking of the birth of a handicapped child loss of dreams is mentioned by the parents as is loss of self-esteem, loss of security, loss of faith. The loss of hopes can be so profound that the name chosen for the child before its birth cannot be used for the handicapped child.

By now it is evident that events involving loss and separation may occur throughout our lives. Though many of these other losses are more frequent than we might at first think, the most extensively studied adult loss has been bereavement and specifically widowhood. For this reason we will present widows' responses to the death of their husbands in considerably

Exercise 3.1 Circumstantial losses

Separation	Blindness
Divorce	Deafness
Emigration	Loss of speech
Burglary	Disfigurement
Stillbirth	Amputation
Miscarriage	Mastectomy
Abortion	Infertility
Death of partner, close friend, member of family	Death of a pet
	Fire
Ageing	Natural disasters
Moving house	Accidents
Imprisonment	Bankruptcy
Birth of a handicapped child	Loss of job
	Retirement
Disability	Leaving home
Rape	Going to school/ college
Sexual abuse	
Hospitalisation	Adoption
Serious illness	Menopause

You will probably think of other circumstantial losses.
Identify how many of these have happened to you.

more detail than widowers' responses. We shall then extend these particular responses to other losses.

One of the major studies was done by Colin Murray Parkes in the late 1960s. He had been so impressed by Charles Darwin's observations on grief in animals, that he drew them to Bowlby's attention. From this there followed a fruitful collaboration, with Parkes deciding to focus on human grief and in particular widowhood. He asked a group of twenty-two

London widows under the age of 65 to tell him in their own words about their bereavement. He saw each widow five times, seeing them at the end of the 1st, 3rd, 6th, 9th and 13th months following bereavement. From this he was able to establish a pattern of 'normal grief' in the first year of bereavement and to discover what factors affected the grieving process. After listening to these widows he was able to see that a clear set of feelings usually emerged.

He must have heard many tales rather like Anne's tale which follows. It is told by a woman about her experience of when her husband died unusually young and just at the point when he was most needed as father of a young child and a new-born baby. It is told verbatim.

'It all started one Whit Monday. I was 25 and my husband, James, was 36. Michael was a small boy of 2 and we were expecting the new baby any day. As we drew into a petrol station my husband casually mentioned that he had found a lump on his shoulder. He sounded casual but somehow I knew it wasn't. My mind raced; was it cancer? a lymphoma maybe? Some of these thoughts were shared as we planned what to do. He must go to the doctor next morning. As a result of the doctor's examination James was admitted to hospital that very Thursday for a biopsy. On the same day I went to another hospital to have the second baby induced. Despite strenuous efforts labour did not start.

What anxious nail-biting days those were. I knew something was seriously wrong with James and yet could get no answer from anyone. James was in another hospital, Michael was at home with my mother and I was alone with my second baby showing no signs of shifting. On the following Tuesday contractions started at last and to my joy James appeared at the hospital about half-an-hour before Pete was born.

There followed a lovely week at home for us all before "all hell let loose". Hell was preceded by a doctor's visit and the casual remark "Oh, by the way, the growth was not highly malignant". This seemed good news. But of course I was clutching at straws. What I heard was the "not malignant", what I failed to hear was the "highly".

So sure was I of a reprieve that I did not believe the hospital's letter, which arrived next day, recalling him for more tests. I even phoned and checked with the GP. Yet within 24 hours James looked desperately ill and the night before returning to hospital insisted on taking me out for a meal, even though he couldn't eat much. When he started telling me where his will was and when the gas and electricity bills needed paying, I had to begin to take on board that he knew he was seriously ill and his insistence was his way of making me face things. I tried to stop him talking this way. I just didn't want to believe what

I was beginning to realise. Within 2 days I knew from my GP that he had inoperable cancer with perhaps only 6 months to live. He knew that he had "some malignancy" which would be reassessed in 6 months. Yet when I approached his bedside the first thing he said was "Sorry I didn't take out that life insurance policy I've been talking about. " By this stage we both knew, at least some of the time, where we were and that he was dying.

The shock left me feeling sick, with loss of memory and appetite, and an inability to sleep. Each night alone in bed I tossed and turned wondering what would happen. Would he die at Christmas? How would I manage? I had two tiny boys, how would they manage? Would I marry again? What would dying be like? Would he die peacefully or in great pain? Did he know I loved him? Could I get a job? Was it my fault? I didn't sleep much in those weeks and frequently cried for much of the night.

When James came out of hospital a fortnight later it was obvious that he was going downhill rapidly. I asked friends and family to come and see us. After his parents had left he told me he had given them our slide projector. At that moment I was suddenly so furious with him that I didn't know what to do with myself. Rather than hit out at him I rushed out and disappeared down the garden knowing he couldn't reach me. Later that night I was able to apologise and we were then able to talk for several hours. We had sensible discussions about what I would do after he died and about those mundane things such as insurance, mortgages and electricity bills. We also talked about the unknown future for both of us. Oddly to me, we also talked of the holiday in 6 months' time which we both knew we would not go on together.

After a few hours' sleep I woke up to find that James was much weaker, he could no longer talk easily. We had done our talking just in time. He was so bad I realised that if James was to be at Pete's christening it would have to be very soon. By noon the christening was arranged for that afternoon. The family all came and the neighbours provided an iced christening cake and the vicar christened Pete in the garden.

All this time James knew he had cancer, but within 4 weeks we both had had to face the fact that death was imminent. Indeed, it was just over 8 weeks from finding the secondary and 3 days after the christening to James's death. In spite of the shock and disbelief 8 weeks earlier, I felt immense relief when, 8 hours before he died, the doctor suggested that James would not live much longer. He was right. As James died at 6.00 a. m. next morning I kissed him goodbye, feeling a great peace and a sense of rightness. Within hours this had been replaced by numbness. It felt as though there was a great distance between me and everyone else, as if I was cocooned in cotton wool. Literally numb with shock; no tears, no feelings, just absolute numbness.

This lasted for a fortnight and was one of the many sensations which made me wonder if I was going crazy. The funeral passed with almost no feeling, and the following 2 weeks in my parents' house passed in a kind of haze. Tears broke through briefly as I tried to respond to the many letters of condolence. Surprisingly this numbness did not seem to affect my ability to do things. I looked after the children, made curtains for my mother, cooked, and yet everything was far away.

I returned to my own house after a fortnight. It was then I started to cry and my mind began to run in overdrive. Any quiet moment was interrupted by endless thoughts, a non-stop nightmare of searching and recall. I remembered all the weeks before James died in minute detail. I remembered events and conversations. I worried about what I hadn't done and had done. My brain just would not "shut down" unless I was frantically busy with something else. This searching around in my mind lasted about 6 months and was relieved occasionally by being able to say it all out loud to someone else. As time went by I became more and more unreasonable with everything and everyone. The slightest difficulty and I blew up, cross with everyone and anyone and often extremely catty. Finally, after about 3 months as I drove along a winding lane I said out loud to James, "You have the better deal. Look what you've left me with." I then thought the answer was to drive into the wall ahead and I would also be fine. Yet almost in the same instance I knew I couldn't. I couldn't do that with the children in the back of the car. This did not stop the anger but gradually I knew I was angry with James for baling out on me.

Though I always knew James was dead, and seeing him dead confirmed that, I still did not believe it. Many was the time when I heard his car draw up and his footsteps coming to the back door. Over a year after he died I saw him in the street. I knew it wasn't James and yet I had to make that stranger talk to convince myself. Each time I knew he was there and yet I knew he was dead. "Was I going mad?" was a frequent question. I felt so silly.

I was also dogged by feelings of guilt. "Wasn't I a beast for going down the garden?" "It was my fault he had died." "I deserved that punishment." "If only I'd done more for him." "If only I'd told him once more that I loved him."

As time passed I felt increasingly lonely and despairing, though after about 6 months my brain was no longer in overdrive. It seemed that every good day was followed by five bad days. I felt like half a person and was very aware of being half a couple. I knew for certain that people only invited me out because they were sorry for me. People didn't really want to see me, or were only being kind, or so I thought.

Of course each "celebration" was hard. The birthdays, Christmas and Easter made me acutely aware of James's absence. Each time there were family and friends to talk to which eased the pain, because something shifted into place, and yet there was still more to be said. But as the first anniversary of James's death loomed I realised that there were now some days which were almost "normal" with no tears, anger or guilt. I realised I hadn't apparently thought of James for several days on end. I discovered that although I hadn't thought of him, I hadn't forgotten him. In a funny way I seemed to remember him better and could talk about him more easily. And so I moved into the second year with more hope than despair.'

In thinking about Anne's story there are actually three adult experiences described. James's experience of dying and leaving a young wife and two babies; Anne's experience of James dying and leaving her alone with two babies and Anne's experience of bereavement. In Exercise 3.2 we invite you to list as many feelings and beliefs as you can from the three angles.

Exercise 3.2   Experiences of the 'letting-go' process

James's experience of facing death	*Anne's experience of facing James's death*	*Anne's experience of bereavement*

How many feelings and beliefs can you find in Anne's story for these three different experiences?

We want to highlight some particular feelings and experiences so clearly expressed in this story. The first is how disbelief and denial emerged for both James and Anne when James was dying and for Anne as she grieved. Anne seemed at one and the same time to deny the severity of James's illness (e.g. 'clutching at straws'), as well as to face the reality of the speed with which James was dying and manage what needed to be done (e. g. get the baby born and christened). James too could deny the proximity of death, while at the very same time face its reality (e. g. talk of the holiday never to be taken, coincident with the discussion of what Anne would do when he died). After his death Anne partly knew James was dead for ever and yet simultaneously heard his footsteps, even saw him in the street, as though a part of her would not give him up.

We can also see how anger and guilt feature in all three experiences. James's first response to hearing his 'death sentence' was to apologise for not having the life insurance sorted out. This seems to indicate a feeling of guilt which, typical of guilt in response to loss, was inappropriate as he had in fact sorted out adequate life cover. We can understand his giving away of something precious to both of them without consultation, as an angry gesture towards Anne. Anne's much more obvious expression of anger was probably a combination of appropriate anger about the non-consultation and loss of the projector, but also an unconscious expression of the under-lying and unacknowledgeable layer of anger with James for abandoning her through his imminent death. We see an expression of her guilt that lonely night when Anne was alone at home and James was in hospital. She kept asking herself 'Was it my fault?'. Having been angry with all and sundry and come to the point of suicidal thoughts, she was at last able to recognise her anger with James for leaving her and having the 'easier' solution. Her guilt again found expression after James's death in her constant self-questioning (e.g. 'Could I have done more?' and 'If only I'd...'). This kind of self-questioning and expression of feeling is completely natural for us all and Anne was lucky enough to have the capacity to express her grief and not deny it. This capacity will have been the result of her early environment, where it was possible to express feelings. Her own ability to grieve, together with the consistent support of family and friends, enabled her to survive and very gradually grow through what had initially looked like a completely impossible situation. The support given to her allowed her to express the different feelings at her own pace and thus helped her to work through her grief and regain her self-esteem.

When a person has a less developed capacity to grieve and the surround-ing community is less supportive, it will be more difficult to get through the grieving process. This is where a counsellor's task would be to recognise the validity of the feelings being expressed and to notice which emotions are being denied. The most likely emotions to be absent are guilt and anger, the ones that are highlighted in Anne's story. We consider ways of working with anger and guilt in chapters 12 and 13.

If we now turn to another story some differences emerge, many of which are typical of the ways in which men and women tend to respond differently to bereavement. As you read Geoff's story, told verbatim of Laura's death, you may notice that the story is told more directly and energetically. Geoff reacts much more practically, his anger is tangible in the very way the story is told. His story shows his acute awareness of the loss of his sexual partner, Laura, and it also highlights the intensity of his sexual responses.

'Laura had been an asthmatic since childhood so when we married I was aware that there was always going to be a problem. When our first child Julie was being born in hospital, Laura had a protracted labour and also serious breathing difficulties. With Christine, born almost 4 years later, it had been touch and go due to a retained placenta and much loss of blood. After that experience Laura had opted for stronger stuff and so, except whilst carrying Gail, had been on a steroid drug for some years. This had greatly improved her quality of life. Her asthmatic attacks, though still occasional, were less intense and not as debilitating. Usually they were confined to times of high stress or monthly periods.

I knew that Laura was a bit below par, so was not surprised when I said, "I was off for a jog", that she replied by saying, "I'll have an early bath and go to bed". On returning from my run I had a drink of water and allowed my breathing to return to normal before going up for a bath. She was in bed as I undressed and had my bath. As I was towelling I heard her go to the lavatory. Almost immediately there was a bump and I rushed in to find her slumped against the door, white as a sheet and apparently unconscious.

My mind was clear. I must move her up with my shoulder, and get her to the bedroom floor before a) starting artificial respiration, b) calling my good friend John from across the road, c) dialling 999 for help, d) waking Julie who was almost 13. As I moved Laura and carried her in my arms I noticed a bruise starting to form on her forehead. I rationalised the priority into: shout for Julie; phone John; start respiration. And so it was. But Julie didn't appear, it was Gail, who was 6. She slept in the room next door and came to see what was going on. I got her to go down and unlock the back door for John, all the while counting and mouth-to-mouth resuscitating. I don't know how long it was before John arrived – probably 3 or 4 minutes. I was tiring. John took over mouth to mouth and I phoned for the ambulance. We continued, taking it in turns. The chest was moving all right, the airways were clear, we sweated with fear and prayed aloud for help, inspiration, anything. Gail was a shadowy little figure in the doorway about 12 feet away, watching wide-eyed – we'd no time to talk and explain – her mother was dying or dead, and we couldn't say anything to her which would make sense.

The ambulance men arrived complete with oxygen. We knew it was hopeless and so did they, but they tried. They asked when she'd last breathed, it was about 15 minutes earlier. I knew enough to realise that even if they'd managed to get oxygen in now it would be too late to be of use. They said sorry and could they use the telephone. The police arrived, alerted by the 999 emergency, and one of them knocked the dinner gong with his helmet. Julie and Christine slept on unaware. I was angry with them for not waking, but it was unreasonable and I knew that. We left them sleeping. Enough time for tears before breakfast.

We all had a cup of tea whilst waiting for the undertaker. Laura upstairs, alone. When the undertakers arrived I took them up. They asked me if I would like to take off her wedding ring. I can't remember who did. It is still around somewhere.

Two or 3 hours after Laura died, it was the middle of the night. John read a story to Gail, inappropriately the one about wolves eating children up. Gail didn't cry but John did. She went to sleep. John offered to stay with me but I declined this kindness, knowing that his wife would be desperate for comfort and intelligence. Laura and she had been good friends. I lay on the bed and thought. I wondered who to tell first and when. I thought about how we'd manage over the next few hours, days, weeks, months. I didn't sleep. At 7.00 a.m. I rose and got Christine to come with Gail and me to Julie's room. Then I told them with Gail joining in the story. It must have been an "impossible" shock and I did wonder whether, I still do wonder, was I right to leave them asleep? We had a weep, then Christine said it was the school photograph that morning so must wash her hair. She did and went to school. We have that photograph.

Julie didn't go to school, but helped me with the other two. She made breakfast whilst I phoned Laura's parents, my parents, close friends and set up the chain to inform as many as possible before they would read it in the paper. A lot to do – no time to grieve. Julie came to work with me before we went to the coroner's office and the doctor's. Then the family started arriving. They were more emotional than we were. Everyone was kind. Few knew how to react to the news. We helped them over the first few sentences, then perhaps we would cry a little. The letters started. Some were horrible and commercial. No doubt all were well meant. They kept on coming for weeks, months even. Julie and I would discuss whether we were strong enough that day to read any, in case they were moving, causing either tears or anger. We read them all – eventually.

In those first few weeks after Laura died I kept busy, there was masses to do. I still had a job, a good job, and I didn't want to jeopardise that. We worked out a routine. Friends and neighbours and relations helped us establish a pattern of life, which enabled a few minutes of calm to pierce the frenetic activity. Sometimes there used to be grief and tears, and often they occurred when least expected. Several times in a line of traffic I would have to pull in when an advertisement, a tune on the radio, one of Laura's favourite songs, would fill me up and I would heave with sobbing, quite unable to drive. I'd resume my journey a few minutes later, curiously refreshed by the emotion.

Several times I would hallucinate. In bed was worst. One side was cold – so cold. As winter drew on I'd put two pillows where once she had lain. I'd wake up convinced she was next to me, and then I would cry and sob with anger when it was a pillow. More than once I was making love to her, passionately, not waking until after the orgasm – my thighs wet, just as they had been as a fantasising teenager. This was no fantasy. I had made love to her again. I did love her. But I'd not said goodbye – no one had. What a lonely way to die, just falling off the loo.'

The sudden ending of this story perhaps reflects the suddenness of Laura's death. This left Geoff with a painfully unfinished relationship and the deep sadness of not having said a mutual goodbye. This sudden bereavement is different from Anne's but nevertheless many of the differences in emotional response seem to be similar to the observation made by Beverley Raphael (1984) when she states that 'the external manifestations of grief may differ because of sex role differences in behaviour'. Our own observations are that men seem to need to regain control of their world more quickly, are more immediately in touch with intense sexual feeling and are also aware of the threat to their sexuality which loss of a partner can pose. They may describe themselves as feeling emasculated or even castrated. Men more often find it difficult to express the sadness of grief and in most cultures it is the women who do the wailing.

From these two stories we could make the observation that the 'single' event of each bereavement contains multiple losses for that person. James's death meant for Anne, at a practical level, the loss of a partner, a father for her children and much else besides. Similarly there were multiple losses for Geoff. We have listed the multiple losses of Anne and Geoff in Table 3.1.

Table 3.1 Multiple losses

Anne's losses	Geoff's losses
1 Partner/companion/help-mate	1 Partner/companion/help-mate
2 Father to children	2 Sexual partner
3 Breadwinner	3 Mother to children
4 Sexual partner	4 Home manager
5 Link with the outside world	

We have chosen the numerical order to signify the priority they gave to the losses. For others the death of a partner might mean the loss of a car-driver, a party-giver, a do-it-yourself expert, a cook, etc. Each of these separate losses needs to be recognised and grieved as an integral part of the total loss.

We have just highlighted some differences between the responses of women and men, but observations show how basically similar the underlying pattern of response to grief is for both men and women. This underlying pattern for women was recorded by Parkes when he studied the feelings of the London widows. He found that there were four phases to mourning with associated feelings, all of which can be found in the stories of Anne and Geoff. In Table 3.2 we summarise the phases and associated feelings and experiences.

Table 3.2   Phases of adult mourning and related feelings

Phases	Predominant feelings
1 Numbness	Shock Disbelief
2 Yearning	Reminiscence Searching Hallucination Anger Guilt
3 Disorganisation and despair	Anxiety Loneliness Ambivalence Fear Hopelessness Helplessness
4 Reorganisation	Acceptance Relief

These phases do not occur one after another but overlap. The feelings often associated with one phase are sometimes associated with another phase as well. We can move from one phase to the next and then back again. Thus when we are grieving we can begin to recognise and take on board the reality of our loss and to experience the associated despair. Then hope seems to spring again and we move back into experiencing yearning, but then back again into despair, when all hope of retrieving the loved one is lost. The way in which these phases are experienced is different for each individual and relates to the uniqueness of each person and their personal life-history. In looking back again at Anne's and Geoff's stories you can perhaps see the interplay of their individual experiences with the basic pattern.

31

Just as the phases are experienced differently for each individual so the time scale also varies. As a rough guide the numbness frequently wears off within a month, the yearning phase diminishes over about 6 months, whereas feelings of disorganisation and despair persist for most of the first year. For many bereaved the grieving proceeds so that acceptance gradually occurs and with this a reorganisation of one's life and beliefs. As a result, by the end of 2 years the majority of bereaved will talk in terms of feeling content or settled and able to feel the normal highs and lows of life and of living.

For a bereavement counsellor it is important to know the phases of mourning and be able to link these with the feelings experienced in a person's story. It is also important to remember that each individual experiences the feelings at their own pace and in their own way and that each bereavement is likely to contain multiple losses for that person.

SUMMARY

1 Circumstantial losses can become sources of personal growth and maturity.
2 The most studied circumstantial loss is the loss of widowhood.
3 The stories of the bereaved are varied and contain intense feelings.
4 Parkes identified a pattern in these feelings that showed four phases of mourning: numbness; yearning; disorganisation and despair; reorganisation.
5 Men and women may have slightly different responses within the four phases of mourning. The phases do not necessarily occur in a linear fashion and both the pace and the overall time scale vary.
6 With any single loss multiple losses occur.

4

THE EFFECT OF EXTERNAL CIRCUMSTANCES AND INTERNAL FACTORS ON THE EXPERIENCE OF BEREAVEMENT

Parkes's study of widows did not stop at simply identifying the four phases of mourning. He observed that the outcome of the grief is affected by certain factors in such a predictable way that they can be called *determinants* of grief. Some of these determinants not only make the grief more complicated but also more prolonged. These determinants have been usefully summarised by Worden (1983) and in this chapter we shall focus on the determinants themselves. In section IV we will consider ways of working with people grappling with some of these particularly complicated kinds of grief.

We have split these determinants into two main groups, external circumstances surrounding the death and the personal history of the bereaved or 'internal factors'. These two main groups have then been further subdivided.

EXTERNAL DETERMINING CIRCUMSTANCES

The external circumstances surrounding the death are summarised in Table 4.1 on the following page.

The place of death will affect the course of grief. For instance, where a person has died far away from home it is easier to deny the death and imagine they will return, as expected, from their journey. This results in prolonged grief. This will be prolonged even further when the dead person's body has not been seen, because it is even easier to deny the death and so postpone or even inhibit grieving. To try and circumvent this problem with men lost in war the Forces have coined the expressions 'missing, presumed dead' and 'lost at sea'. These phrases try to encompass the difficult situations of not knowing if someone is dead and not seeing the dead person.

Coincidental loss refers to losses occurring simultaneously, as in a car

33

Table 4.1 External determining circumstances affecting grief

1	Place of death	Where a person has died in a faraway place, then the acceptance of the death will be postponed and the grief will take longer.
2	Coincidental deaths or losses	Where there are simultaneous deaths in a family or community, then grief is more complex and there is less comfort and support available.
3	Successive deaths or losses	When losses, deaths or disaster follow one another in quick succession then the grief over the one may be distracted or disturbed by the shock and grief of the next one.
4	The nature of the death	Where a death is untimely or sudden, it is more difficult to grieve. Where a sudden death is also traumatic or horrendous, it is even more difficult to grieve.
5	Social networks	a) Close knit and mutually helpful communities and families will be particularly useful at the time of bereavement or loss. b) For different groups at different times in history, ideas about and attitudes and behaviour towards death and dying are different. Some groups are more accepting and recognising of death and dying people and therefore they are less likely to deny and more likely to facilitate grief (see chapters 6 and 7).

accident for instance, where two members of a family are killed and maybe a third injured. Here the survivor's grief is usually prolonged. These coincidental losses render the griever particularly vulnerable as the different losses each need to be individually grieved. Further, the expected sources of support themselves may be severely reduced through injury or even the death itself.

Other examples might be families caught up in a major disaster such as the Blitz or the Holocaust or more recently the several major disasters which have occurred in the 1980s. If, for instance, people from three generations have died then the survivors have little support. An example might be a woman whose husband, father and daughter have died. In order to grieve the death of her husband she might need the support of her mother, but her mother has just been widowed and has her own grief to deal with. In order to grieve her daughter, she would need the support of her husband, but he too is dead, and even her sister-in-law is in grief for her own brother. Her own sister is grieving for her father, as is her nephew of whom she was particularly fond, having been unable to have a son of her own. Her 'task' is to grieve each of the people she has lost, but the resources in the way of family to help her through the long processes of grief are severely depleted. If the whole community is grieving then the complications facing each individual griever may be even more enormous, with both the family and community network unavailable. In this sort of circumstance grieving will go on for many years and can pass from one generation to the next.

Another external circumstance, which complicates the grieving process, occurs when deaths or other losses happen in quick succession, so that the griever does not have time to grieve the first loss before the second one is upon her. For an individual this might occur when a parent dies a few days after the last child has left the parental home; or when a house move follows within a few weeks of a separation or divorce.

There seem to be reduced resources to begin to grieve the second loss, which is often put aside or denied. It is then difficult to resurrect and grieve this second loss until the first loss has been worked through. This probably also happens at national level when disasters happen in close succession.

The nature of a death or loss will also affect the way in which it is grieved. Where a death is untimely and unexpected or sudden, then it is harder to accept that the death has actually taken place and is therefore harder to grieve. This may well be because the death is 'unthinkable', which makes it harder to believe. It is as though it becomes, at least for a time, 'unfeelable' as well. An example might be of a child dying before her parents. In the natural order of things we expect to die before our children, so a child's death is unthinkable. This frequently results in a prolongation of the grieving.

Prolongation is often even more pronounced where death has been through suicide or homicide. It will be no surprise that the feelings associated with grieving for someone who has been murdered or killed can seem overwhelming. There will be intense anger, vengeful thoughts and fantasies of revenge directed towards the killer or murderer. Where the killer cannot be identified the fantasies may well be greater and the grief more difficult. Often people feel unable to express these feelings and thoughts. Encouragement to express them and recognise their validity is essential.

In grieving a suicide the mixed feelings are frequently very intense, volatile and difficult to bear. One moment there is intense anger at someone killing themselves that way, the next moment overwhelming sorrow that the person felt there was no way out but to kill themselves, and at yet the very next moment extreme guilt at having not heard the person's cry for help nor managed to save them. This alternation of feelings can be quite overwhelming and make the grieving process considerably more tortuous. The sense of punishment is often all-pervading. The 'survivors' of the suicide have not been able to prevent the death and think they should have seen the signs and been able to do something. In fact some 'successful' suicides do not ask for help and their signals of despair have been deeply hidden, perhaps because those around found it difficult to respond to such deep feelings of despair. It may be that it was this very inability to recognise and show their own needs that was one of the fundamental problems for the suicide and their relatives. The bereaved person in this instance will find anger particularly difficult to express. This gives the counsellor an important role in giving permission for the angry feelings to exist and be expressed.

Death through suicide or homicide also falls into the unthinkable category and again we tend to deny the unthinkable. This denial is further complicated when the survivors have not seen the body, either because there is no body to see or because the body is so badly mutilated or decomposed. In this latter case the decision as to whether to see the body or not is a genuinely difficult one. On the one hand the searing images resulting from seeing the mutilated body may be experienced as persecutory, because they will not go away; on the other hand the fantasies that arise from not seeing the body can also be haunting. In either case, this aspect of the grieving will need considerable attention, for the griever will have to acknowledge the unthinkable death and think about the horrific nature of that death. This task is, of course, not unique to homicide and suicide. Accidents and disasters can be equally horrific.

In considering suicide and homicide we have mentioned the haunting images associated with horrific deaths. These vivid images frequently persecute the grievers and survivors of disasters, as well as the helpers involved with the disasters. These different groups may all be persecuted with both nightmares and vivid daytime images, for many months if not years thereafter. This, together with overwhelming feelings of guilt about being a survivor, often lead to a set of symptoms and experiences now described as post traumatic stress disorder (PTSD). This is characterised by psychic numbing, which in severe cases can be intractable, repeated vivid recall of the horrific event and a guilt which is hard to expiate. There is no doubt that most survivors of major disasters, whether personal or national, will need referral to experienced specialist helpers. Recognition of this need has resulted in crisis intervention teams being formed by social services departments and trauma counselling services being set up immediately following a disaster.

The fifth external circumstance mentioned in Table 4.1 is that of the social networks surrounding the bereaved. We have deliberately set this factor apart from the other four in this table and also included it in Table 4.2 (internal factors or personal history of the bereaved). We have included social networks surrounding the bereaved in the external circumstances because where groups remain together and are not separated by the demands of a more mobile society, and where the extended family remains in close geographic proximity, it may be easier to obtain the emotional support required. Immigrants adjusting to new cultures will find it much easier to let go of the old culture and adjust to the new where there are cohesive social networks of support.

Many people nowadays are separated from their families and may well not belong to the community where they live because they come from a different ethnic and cultural or social group. Unfortunately it is common for families not to know their neighbours. All this means that supportive networks are frequently missing just when they are most needed. On the other hand, social networks may be present, but the griever may be unable to use them because they do not know how to make relationships. The inability to make relationships is, of course, to do with their personal history and hence the inclusion of 'social networks' in Table 4.2 (page 38). In either case support is unavailable and the griever will be much more prone to prolonged grieving if not breakdown. This relationship factor will be considered again under internal factors.

Similarly, the influence of society at large and the whole culture externally affect the course of grief but they also interact with our personal history, thus affecting us internally. Every culture has mourning rites and ways of handling a death (chapter 6) which are available to help when someone dies. Families will vary enormously in whether they will observe the rituals of their culture or use them to facilitate grieving. Some families and groups are prone to denial, so there will be little encouragement to the griever to express feelings. Thus denial is compounded rather than challenged. This repression of feelings may well eventually manifest itself in physical or mental illness. The more a particular group in society is likely to repress or deny death, the more likely are its members to have difficulty with grieving.

Although we have specifically highlighted how the social network affects grieving both internally and externally, it is, of course, true to some extent for the other four external circumstances. It is inevitable that how we respond to external circumstances is conditioned by our personal life history and the related internal emotional world (chapter 1).

INTERNAL FACTORS

We have called the personal life history and related internal world, the internal factors affecting the grieving process. Parkes's research confirms that the process of grief is indeed affected by these aspects built up from one's personal life history. These include early attachment experiences and the loss history of the bereaved. Further, the age and life-cycle stage of the griever, the level of intimacy with the lost person and the complexity of the relationship will all likewise affect the grief. This is summarised in Table 4.2 on page 38.

You will remember from chapter 1 and the references to Bowlby's research, that early secure attachments provide inner resources which help us to manage later stressful and threatening situations. Tom had been securely attached to Mary and had begun to assimilate and develop the 'secure base', which he initially experienced in Mary, and then inside himself. He was then able to tolerate her absence. We can predict that, given a reasonable life-history, Tom will be able to express feelings and respond appropriately to grief in adult life. We can further predict that the nursery children in Ainsworth's research, who were insecurely attached, would

Table 4.2   Internal factors affecting grief

1 Attachment history	Where, as a small child, someone has been 'securely attached' and can cope reasonably with anxiety (as outlined in chapter 1), then their capacity to express feelings and work through grief in later life is greater.
2 Loss and death history	Where previous losses have been difficult to accept and grieve, then the current loss may 're-awaken' that earlier loss and render both particularly difficult to grieve.
3 Age and stage of griever	For children and young people and for those passing through particularly vulnerable transition points in the life-cycle, grief may be especially challenging.

These three factors above will affect the individual griever's capacity to grieve any loss.
The following three factors will influence the reaction to the loss of a particular relationship.

4 Intimacy level	The more intimate the relationship to the lost person (spouse, child, lover, parent, sibling, etc.), the more intense the grief. This, too links with the quality of attachment described in chapter 1.
5 Emotional complexity	The more straightforward the relationship the more straightforward the grief. More complex relationships with many denied feelings or unrecognised ambivalence are more complex to grieve.
6 Social networks	a) Close-knit and mutually helpful communities will be particularly useful at the time of bereavement or loss if the griever has the capacity to use them. b) For different groups at different times in history, ideas about and attitudes and behaviour towards death and dying are different. Some groups are more accepting and recognising of death and dying and therefore less likely to deny and more likely to facilitate grief, provided the griever can be helped in this way.

have more difficulty with grief in adult life and, depending on other resources available in their lives, would have more difficulty with the feelings associated with grief.

It is also possible to predict from Parkes's research that when a person, with either insufficient external support and/or internal resources, suffers a major loss through death or separation, they will find it difficult to accept and recognise that loss, with the result that the grieving process may well be incomplete and even blocked. If a new loss then occurs it may well 'reawaken' the earlier loss and the response to that loss may seem 'out of all proportion'. In reality they may be doing double 'grief-work', not unlike the simultaneous losses mentioned in Table 4.1 with the similar task of grieving one loss after the other. The following story illustrates just such a blocking of one loss affecting the grieving of further losses.

Julia (29) was divorced rather quickly, in a flurry of ambivalent feelings. Forced to leave the marital home and with two small children to look after, it was all too easy for her to get caught up with the tasks of establishing a new home, a new career and looking after two children rather than grieving the lost home and relationship. She seemed to be managing well. When, however, a few years later her mother died she was plunged into a deep depression. It was only by being helped to recognise the first loss that she was able to begin the long process of grief for her mother.

A further factor which will affect individuals' capacity to grieve is their age and stage of emotional maturity at the time of the loss and whether or not they are going through a period of transition. Children at different ages have different understandings of death and separation. We refer to young children's grief in more detail in chapter 7.

Adolescence itself is a transition period of loss as well as gain. Adolescents have to grapple with the loss of childhood in order to face the responsibilities as well as the challenges of adulthood. Although some may try to remain Peter Pans for ever, the continual development of their own sexuality will pull them inexorably towards adulthood. This period of adolescence with, on the one hand, its looking back longingly and searching for that which was lost and, on the other, its looking ahead with apprehension to a new world full of unknown challenges is quite like the experience of grief itself. The griever too looks back longingly for that which is lost and fears the inevitable changes which lie ahead. Thus adolescence is a particularly difficult time during which to grieve the loss of a close relationship. In western cultures at least, the task of adolescents is to separate themselves from their family of origin. Inevitably the loss of a family member through death or separation at this stage will make the task even harder.

Another transition period in the life-cycle when individuals are more vulnerable to loss is the time, for adults, when the children have left the family home, and the parents are adjusting to that change in the family group. Women may be particularly vulnerable, both because this period often coincides with menopause and its changes, and because women in our culture are still often more involved than men with the lives and welfare of the children at home. They therefore have more adjusting to do when the children leave. The adjustments required at the transition into retirement also render people vulnerable to other losses.

These three factors, attachment history, loss history and age or stage in the life-cycle, will affect an individual's capacity to grieve whatever losses arise. In addition intimacy and emotional complexity, which are aspects of the relationship which is lost, will also affect the outcome of grief.

The more intimate the relationship to the person who was lost, the more intense the grief. Of course we know this in a common-sense kind of way; it is much worse to lose a husband than to lose the relatively unknown neighbour three doors down the street. Yet there are often dimensions to this aspect of intimacy which go unseen or misunderstood, leaving the griever particularly vulnerable. Frequently a friend or colleague at work could be much closer than a brother or sister. Another example of a particularly intimate relationship might be between a child and her grandparent. This relationship could well go unrecognised by other family members, so the child can be left alone in her unrecognised grief when the grandparent dies, or is effectively lost through a geographic move. The importance of the death of a child's pet may also go unrecognised.

Where the nature of a relationship is not understood or, even worse, largely unaccepted by society, then the griever is often abandoned just at the moment when they most need the help of others. Particular examples of this are gay relationships or extramarital affairs. The following story illustrates the particular problems.

> Elisabeth and Jane had been living together in an intimate relationship for 8 years. They were very close to one another and although they had a number of friends in the small town where they lived and worked, not many people knew about or understood their relationship. Neither of their families accepted their relationship either, and although each one visited her family from time to time, they visited alone. They had agreed not to contact one another at the other's parental home. Elisabeth's parents lived some distance away and she had gone to visit them for a week. She was due back on the Saturday lunch-time. Jane had prepared a lovely meal for her but Elisabeth did not appear. Jane found ways of making sense of this delay but by Saturday evening she was pretty frantic. She managed to hold out until Sunday morning, by which time she could wait no longer. When she rang she was shouted at by Elisabeth's brother, who informed her that Elisabeth was dead and that it was no use ringing now! He then put the phone down. When she rang again to try to find out more, she was told that the funeral was next day, but on no account was her presence sanctioned at that occasion. Jane later learned that Elisabeth had been very badly injured in a car accident the previous Saturday, had been taken to a nearby hospital and died a few days later. Her family had been with her much of the time but she had been too weak to insist on contacting Jane. Thus Jane was left; not able to see Elisabeth in her dying days and make her farewell, not able to go to the funeral, feeling both punished in some way for Elisabeth's death and utterly alone in her grief.

The other aspect of a relationship which affects the process of grief is its emotional complexity. Where a relationship has been reasonably direct, loving and affectionate the grief will be relatively straightforward, however long and intense. Where, however, the relationship has been less direct and open, has been more complicated, and where feelings have been hidden or denied, then the grief will be more complex. The feelings often most hotly denied are those of anger and resentment and when these feelings 'go underground' they are often turned against the self. We consider these denied or repressed feelings in more detail in chapters 12 and 13.

On page 37 we refer to the possibility that even where supportive social networks do exist the griever may be unable to use these because their personal history affects the use which can be made of such networks and rituals. Thus, internal factors can influence the effect of external factors as well as the other way round.

It is not possible to say exactly how these external and internal factors will determine the course of the grief for any one individual. However, in the knowledge of their existence, it is possible to look out for the grieving which seems to be at the extremes of the spectrum outlined in chapter 1. Counsellors should be alert to the possibility of referring to more specialist care those who may be denying the feelings so much that they seem consistently immune to the experience, as well as those showing chaotically disturbed behaviour. In chapter 14 these factors affecting grief are linked to assessment procedures in Table 14.1 (page 154) and then referral procedures are outlined.

SUMMARY

1 Certain factors, known as determinants of grief, affect the outcome of grief.
2 The external factors known to affect grief are: place of death; coincidental deaths; successive deaths; the nature of the death; the social network surrounding the bereaved.
3 The internal factors known to affect grief are: attachment history; loss and death history; age and stage of griever; intimacy level; emotional complexity of the lost relationship; the social network surrounding the bereaved.
4 There is an interrelatedness between external and internal factors.

5

HISTORICAL CHANGE IN ATTITUDES TO DEATH AND BEREAVEMENT

We have considered some different bereavements and the different factors which can affect a person's mourning. We have also looked at how denial functions to protect individuals from the initial impact of the loss, but how it can also prevent people from recognising the loss and doing the work of grief before eventually letting go. It is not just individuals who deny death but whole groups and even societies. By taking a historical perspective it is possible to begin to see how patterns of denial within any one society change over time and also influence the present.

In medieval times death was perceived as a much greater presence than in today's developed societies. This is not surprising given that not only was life expectancy about half what it is today and people had to be prepared to face death after a much shorter life, but also that death was much more likely to be violent, cruel and more physically painful.

Death was unpredictable and uncontrollable. People therefore had to live with a much greater awareness of death around them and of their own mortality. Dead and dying bodies were things which everyone had seen and, given the rate of infant mortality alone, everyone was likely to have lost someone close to them through death. With these constant reminders of death in the midst of life, people could not deny the existence of death in the way we do today, and they were forced to be more prepared to meet their deaths.

But having to face consistently the possibility of one's end and the finiteness of human existence is a hard task. This was mitigated in the Middle Ages by a belief in an afterlife. A belief that death is not the absolute end, and that the soul moves on to another place, or that we are reborn in another form, has given solace to humans everywhere, probably since human beings first became aware of their own mortality. Perhaps these comforting ideas evolved as people realised that death was the inevitable conclusion to life. Awareness of death has always been difficult to bear, and human beings have long grappled with the meaning of the end and with the feelings associated with death. Anger and guilt seem to have been the most difficult of these feelings to understand.

One of the oldest stories of our civilisation is that of Adam and Eve. Freud, amongst others, pointed out the connection here between the fear of death and feelings of guilt. Adam and Eve were innocent and immortal in paradise. However, once they had sinned and violated the commandment of God they became mortal and were condemned to die. The idea that death is a punishment for evil committed has probably contributed to the human fear of death over millennia.

Amongst the strong emotions evoked by death, guilt is almost always experienced. It is an unpleasant feeling and we often rush to find a 'guilty party' or scapegoat to 'carry' any guilty feelings we do not want. In earlier societies a death was often understood as a killing, albeit by nonhuman forces. Even today in relation to our own disasters we can observe how a 'guilty party' is often sought. Sometimes even the victims themselves can become tainted with guilt, through the blaming by those who can find no better way of coming to terms with their own guilt and fear. Today we can observe this in the tendency to blame Aids upon 'promiscuity'. Awareness of this association of guilt and death can perhaps help us to understand the enormous value of the sacraments of confession, forgiveness and absolution. In medieval times when disease rendered death so unpredictable and uncontrollable, the regular rite of absolution must have helped to decrease fear and increase a sense of readiness for death. The sense of guilt and the fear of punishment around death seem to have been more clearly recognised in previous centuries than nowadays. The seeking and granting of absolution went largely unquestioned until the Reformation.

With the Age of Enlightenment scientific understanding grew. Each wave of scientific discovery was followed by biological and medical discoveries. By the end of the nineteenth century both pain and disease were beginning to be controlled. Fewer women died in childbirth, disease had become less random and more controllable through both prevention and cure, and illness had become less painful. Life had become longer, with greater predictability, and death seemed to recede and be more under human control. Gradually it must have seemed as if death itself was controllable. But these great changes were bought at a price.

The major price seems to be that death is denied and 'forgotten about', both at a social as well as at an individual level. In other words death is 'repressed'. Whereas in earlier times death and dying took place in the family circle and for many people within the single, shared family space, now death has become marginalised. Our dying has been more or less 'banned' either to hospital or some other institution or, if at home, then to another room, rather than in the bosom of the family. It is no longer common to see or touch our dead. Their corpses are cared for by others and their graves, if there are graves, are often tended by public services. Not only do we 'not speak ill of the dead', we are hardly able to talk about death and dying at all.

This discomfort about death seems to have led to shame and embarrassment and an avoidance of talking or writing about the stark facts of death and dying. There are quite common words which are spoken in hushed tones or even avoided altogether. For instance a 'growth' is used to describe cancer and 'passed away' for died. By contrast, in seventeenth-century love poetry, death was used as a favourite theme to remind the beloved of the brevity of life and human beauty and hence the folly of delaying love's advances. Were today's lover to write a poem mentioning the future activity of worms in the beloved's grave it would probably meet with considerable distaste if not downright repulsion!

We also seem to have this embarrassment not only in talking about death and dying, but in talking to dying people. Out of sheer awkwardness we may say nothing and keep away. We thus deprive both ourselves and the dying person of touching, of words of comfort and the mutual recognition we all need. Then the very words the dying need to hear, the invaluable proof of our affection and tenderness, go unsaid and unheard.

It is not only the dying from whom we distance ourselves, we also distance ourselves from those who are ageing and infirm and whose mortality is less easily denied. One way of avoiding both their and our mortality is through banishing them to residential homes. Some homes enable the elderly to grieve such losses as independence, professional role and personal privacy, but most homes seem to find difficulty in acknowledging the transition from life to death. Many such homes work on the principle of a firm demarcation of the living from those-about-to-die, as if the former were immortal. They quickly and secretly remove anyone who dies, do not encourage any grieving for their dead and generally refuse to discuss any fears about death and dying (Hockey, 1990). This denial of death is understandably most intense amongst those working with the elderly and with the dying.

At the other end of life we also find adults introducing a process of embarrassed denial with young children. In modern western societies children are rarely given much realistic information about death and, where the topic cannot be avoided, it is often treated in a vague or unrealistic manner. Most children nowadays have not seen a human corpse and we go to enormous lengths to protect them from this sight, often also preventing them from going to an important funeral. Adults, although they talk of 'protecting the children' are, of course, protecting themselves from feelings they find difficult and which the children may express more openly. As we will consider further in chapter 7, adults' denial is the principal difficulty for children who are trying to grapple with death and bereavement.

Another consequence of not speaking about death is that we learn very little about the rituals associated with dying and death. Indeed, our own cultural rituals to aid the transition from life to death seem to be increasingly lost from common knowledge. Frequently there is no one in our local neighbourhood who knows how to lay out the dead and only nurses and undertakers learn how to do this. Thus we hand over rituals, which would be helpful to us, to professionals whom we usually do not know personally.

Not speaking about death also means that there is no common knowledge about the procedures associated with burial and cremation. Thus, for instance, we may not know that we can indicate to the undertaker what should be done with someone's ashes. One of our bereaved acquaintances was recently shocked when the urn containing the ashes was delivered to her house. She simply did not know what to do with the ashes. This kind of 'not-knowing' renders us powerless and we tend to believe that the professionals are the only ones who can manage the transition from life to death. We therefore dissociate ourselves further from the valuable rituals and this 'ignorance' in turn feeds the general denial of death. The cycle of denial then becomes increasingly hard to break.

There are, however, signs that this trend towards denial is beginning to reverse. During the last 25 years there seems to have been a trend towards a greater openness about death and dying. Writers such as John Hinton, Elisabeth Kübler-Ross, John Bowlby, Colin Murray Parkes, Beverley Raphael, and Rosemary and Victor Zorza have played an important part in this. Also the work of Cecily Saunders and the hospice movement, in introducing and supporting greater openness about death and the feelings associated with dying, have made it possible for many more people to die in relatively little pain and in an open and supportive relationship with their families and close friends.

A recent research study into homes and hospices by Jennifer Hockey (1990) describes this openness in hospices. She traces the idea of a hospice to the early Christian attitude of unconditional love and recognises that it is a form of hospitality that existed well before modern hospitals with their regimented admission procedures. Her exploration reveals how the strict boundary between life and death, imposed by most residential homes and hospitals, is gradually being eroded within the hospice. This enables each individual to choose his or her own personal level of denial and to manage his or her own transition from healthy adult, through the phase of being sometimes healthy and sometimes ill, to ill person and then to dying person. This more fluid system of recognition and support through the transition period has in turn much influenced the management of death in some hospitals and general practices. Time will tell how far this trend towards openness can counter the trend towards almost total denial, to achieve a more useful balance between denial and recognition for both individuals and society. Of course the denial of death is a necessary part of the grief process, but there is also a time when we or others need to talk about it.

We need to recognise the value of beliefs and rituals to help the dying, and those who are close to them, through this momentous transition. In the next chapter we look at the cultural rituals that exist in Britain today. Many of these will be unfamiliar to us, not so much because they are forgotten, but because Britain is multi-ethnic and consists of a rich variety of groups, each with their unique history and culture. A knowledge of the enormous variety of mourning rituals is essential to any loss counsellor.

SUMMARY

1 In earlier centuries death was more 'present' in people's lives and it was harder to deny its presence. It was also seen as less predictable and people were more ready for death in the midst of life.
2 Death has always been associated with guilt, and blame has been apportioned in different ways. Rituals of absolution help to relieve the dying of burdens of guilt and blame.
3 Medical advances in the last 150 years have 'banished' death from our midst. This has been accompanied by increased denial of death and decreased ability to accept or talk about death, even with the dying themselves.
4 Death is unknown and the fear of death leads, understandably, to a denial of death. The recognition and acceptance of death can enhance life and certainly eases the experience of the dying.
5 Patterns of denial and acceptance change over time. The trend towards denial in western societies seems to have slowed and there are signs of a growing acceptance of death.

6

CULTURAL VARIETY
Shared elements

THE VALUE OF MOURNING

In chapter 4 we observed how the social network surrounding the bereaved is one of the external factors affecting the course of grief. Different social networks and different cultural groups deal with grief in different ways. We also noted that every culture has mourning rites and ways of handling a death. However, families and individuals vary in how much they are able to use the networks available to them, and also in how much they observe the rituals. In this chapter we focus on the value of mourning rituals and on the many different kinds current in Britain today.

Attitudes to death in human societies are almost infinitely varied, as anthropologists and archaeologists have helped to show. Whatever the rituals, however, the emotions of loss and disturbance are much the same. Bowlby (1980) in his wide-ranging quest to understand more about the human response to death studied the work of a number of anthropologists. Drawing on Malinowski (1925), Firth (1961) and others he writes of the common functions of funerals across a range of societies. Although funerals are for the dead they actually fulfil various functions for the living. These include helping the bereaved to recognise that the loss has indeed occurred, and providing a place for the expression of grief. Firth also postulates that the funeral enables other members of the community to take public note of their loss, to say farewell and to express, in a prescribed way, the powerful feelings of fear and anger often engendered by the death. In addition the funeral and funeral gifts express, even if only symbolically, the cohesiveness of the group and their willingness to help one another in times of adversity.

Bowlby reflects further that a funeral also offers an opportunity for the living to express their gratitude to the deceased and to take action felt to be for the benefit of the recently deceased person. The bereaved themselves are recognised by virtually all societies to be in need and in a state of shock and disorientation. This in turn elicits, almost universally, certain responses to the bereaved such as care, feeding, support and comfort.

Bowlby reports from his study that although cultural patterns of grief and mourning differ enormously in their particular ceremonies and in what is encouraged and what is denied, virtually all of them have rules and rituals relating to the following three elements:

1   how a continuing relationship with the dead person should be conducted in the mourning period;
2   how blame should be allocated and anger expressed;
3   how long mourning should last.

We might assume, therefore, that there is a human need to manage the difficult period after the death; to express the anger evoked by death and to allocate the associated blame; and to define a period of mourning which, through its ending, gives permission or enables the bereaved to return fully to the community. It also helps to mark the change or transition. Referring to these elements Bowlby asserts, 'In these ways a culture channels the psychological responses of individuals and in some degree ritualises them. The origins of the responses themselves lie, however, at a deeper level.' Bowlby's fascinating accounts of grief in very different cultures can be read in chapter 8 of his volume on *Loss*.

This short résumé of the anthropologists' findings has been included because it highlights the ways in which beliefs and rituals help us to take leave of the dying and the dead, and set a term to the period of mourning.

Sadly, rituals which were helpful and useful to the generation of our grandparents and even to our parents, may still be disappearing. Rituals help us through difficult changes. They supply specific words and actions which have meanings of great value to those who share in the ritual, and they can help us to say goodbye and make an end to a relationship. Rituals (such as shutting the eyes of the dead person, stopping the clocks, wearing black or a black armband, drawing the curtains during day and night) help us to acknowledge the death and facilitate grieving. Similarly the Jewish customs of the 7 days (*shiva*), the 30 days (*shiloshim*), and the setting of the stone after a year help to mark the periods of grief.

MOURNING IN DIFFERENT CULTURAL AND RELIGIOUS GROUPS

Britain is now a multicultural society where different cultural and religious groups have different rituals. Some have retained a much richer set of responses and rituals to help them through the process of dying and grieving. In working with people from a variety of cultural groups whose sociocultural background may be unfamiliar to us, we need to recognise both the value of all mourning rituals and also the range and variety of different rituals in the different groups within our society.

Where groups remain together and are not separated by the demands of a more mobile society, and where the extended family remains in close geographic proximity, it may be easier to fulfil the rituals available and to offer the emotional support required. But many people nowadays are separated from their families, may well not belong to the community where they live and may pay less heed to their own rituals. All this means that supportive networks and the concomitant rituals are frequently missing just when we need them most. Without the support of rituals and emotional connections we are much more prone to prolonged grieving if not breakdown. What is needed most of all is emotional support, for this enables us to talk. Where the expression of grief is not encouraged and where denial is given priority, then feelings are repressed. This repression may well eventually manifest itself in physical or mental illness. The more a particular group in society is likely to repress or deny death, the more likely are its members to have difficulty with grieving.

We believe that those working within our multiracial society, particularly in the areas of death and bereavement, will need to be aware of those different beliefs, different attitudes to human life and death and of the great range of rituals associated with death and bereavement. It is also important to recognise the way in which the various beliefs and rituals will have separate meanings for each individual within any given 'group' or religion. It is all too easy to jump to conclusions or make assumptions. When someone filling in a form writes 'Hindu', for instance, there will be as many individual meanings of that word 'Hindu' as form-fillers. For any one individual writing 'Jew' as their 'religious affiliation' there are many things we do not know. We do not, for instance, know whether they are liberal-reform or orthodox Jews, or are from a Sephardic or Ashkenazi tradition. Neither would we know what that person's individual beliefs were concerning the afterlife, nor indeed whether their religious beliefs mean very much to them at all. Furthermore their feelings about their religion, or their belonging to that religious group, would be unknown to us. It is important, therefore, to develop a sensitivity towards the concerns of the individual as well as towards the possible requirements of their faith. This can be achieved by having some knowledge of the culture and religion from which he or she comes, as well as some awareness of the different sects and varieties within that group.

In a book of this size it is, of course, impossible to give anything but the most cursory description of the great religions of the world, all of which are represented in Britain today. What we have chosen to highlight and to try to summarise are the beliefs about death and an afterlife and about the customs and practices in relation to the dying and the bereaved for each of the major religions. However, there are many people who profess no religious beliefs and yet who are required by law to bury or cremate their dead. They may or may not seek some ceremonial recognition of the transition from life to death. We have therefore added a short section on some of the procedures available to them, and some of the difficulties that can arise.

Judaism

The fundamental tenet could be summed up as follows; trust in a single, invisible external God who created the world. Jews can relate directly to God and their relationship with God is depicted as a combination of defiance and acceptance. Rather than a creed or doctrine, Judaism stresses right behaviour which includes supporting one another. Views about the afterlife are very varied and often rather vague. Judaism is life-affirming and there is great emphasis on the here-and-now. Life now is highly valued and there are very strict rules about not shortening a person's life.

Resting on the sabbath (sundown Friday to sundown Saturday) is an important custom for many Jews. Even though Jews are commanded to bury their dead as quickly as possible, a body cannot be moved on the sabbath and, usually, someone stays with the body until the funeral. For orthodox Jews, burial is essential whilst for some liberal Jews cremation is also a possibility. Kaddish, a prayer affirming life and praising God, is recited by the mourners at the time of death and at the stone-setting after one year.

After the funeral the mourners will 'sit *shiva*', that is, sit on a low chair, in the house of the dead and not be involved in any activity. People who knew the dead person or know the bereaved are duty-bound to visit, bringing food as well as comfort and support. For most bereaved people it is a very valuable experience to have the company of people ready to listen to their agony and talk of the one who has died. It is also psychologically useful for it encourages people to express their grief. A stone is set at the grave on the first anniversary of the death; an important ceremony, which helps the griever through this difficult anniversary.

The most intensive period of grief is the first 7 days (*shiva*). The next 30 days (*shiloshim*) mark a period of lesser intensity. After a year the bereaved may let go of their grief and remarry if they are ready.

The 'rending of garments' originally expressed the passion of grief. This may still happen nowadays but it is generally more ceremonial with the snipping of a man's lapel with scissors or wearing a torn garment. Symbolically, however, this gives expression to the powerful, indeed rending feelings, associated with grief.

Christianity

In common with Judaism and Islam, Christianity believes there is only one God; unlike the other monotheistic religions, Christians believe that God has come on earth in human form through Jesus Christ (Christos = Messiah) and through the Holy Spirit as his spiritual force moving in all people. Christianity has many sects and variations, some placing greater emphasis on a literal interpretation of the scriptures than others.

The afterlife is a firm part of Christian belief, but the way in which it is viewed varies from a belief in a different kind of existence for the soul, after separation from the body, to a less dualistic idea of bodily resurrection in some form. Some will have a literal view of hell and heaven, while others may understand these words in a more symbolic way. At the time of death there is often a reflection on the life lived on earth, but also a seeking of that other dimension of life which is not terminated by physical death. Some may accept death as part of the will of God, while others will view it with fear, anger and disillusionment. It is important to explore these feelings and to remember that some people can find renewed faith and trust as they approach death, whilst for the disillusioned, faith is not a comfort.

The three main groups of Christians are the Orthodox, Catholic and Protestant. Orthodox Christians usually wish a priest to hear a last confession and give communion before death. There is often a lying-in in the church so that family and friends can pay their last respects and make their farewells before burial. Catholic Christians also lay great emphasis on the 'sacrament of the sick', 'extreme unction' or 'last rites' when confession is made, absolution given and communion is taken. There is usually a lying-in period for farewells followed by burial or cremation. Within the Protestant tradition there are fewer formally observed 'last rites', although many practising Anglicans may wish to receive the sacrament of the sick before death. Practice varies in relation to the lying-in and saying farewell. Cremation is more common now than burial within the Protestant group although again practice varies. Christian families of whatever denomination frequently follow the burial or cremation with a gathering of family and friends of the deceased.

The variety of belief amongst Christians is very wide. For most Christians, however, the belief in an afterlife with a sense of being united with relatives or friends and of a fuller relationship with God can help to ease the pain of accepting death. A strong religious faith is sometimes helpful for people approaching death but anger with God, about an untimely death for instance, is often particularly difficult for bereaved Christians to bear.

Islam

The fundamental tenet of Islam is also that there is one true God: 'Islam' means 'submission' to God's will. The prophet Muhammed is the messenger of the one true God. The Koran contains a record of Muhammed's teaching which, combined with his sayings and deeds, makes up the Islamic legal system. Thus there is no division between secular and religious law. Faith, prayer, fasting, giving alms and pilgrimage is the duty of everyone within the Islamic community.

It is important before Ramadan, the period of fasting, that Moslems sort out disputes, problems and ill-feelings. Where death comes in or around Ramadan this is a period of particularly intense personal sorting out.

Like Christians and some Jews, Moslems believe in life after death as one stage in God's overall plan for humanity. The death of a loved one, therefore, is seen as a temporary separation and part of God's will. However difficult, the separation is to be accepted with a surrendering to His will.

The family pray at the bedside of a dying person, whose head should be turned towards Mecca. Once dead the family wash and lay out the body. It is important to remember that non-Moslems should not touch the body; if moving the body is a necessity, then wearing a pair of gloves is an acceptable solution. Moslems are buried, never cremated, and this should be within 24 hours. The body is taken to the mosque or graveside for prayers before burial in an unmarked grave. The body is normally wrapped in a special cloth rather than placed in a coffin. Coffins and marked graves are a requirement in Britain, which may make things particularly difficult for Moslems in this country.

Although some very pious Moslems may exercise great constraint over the expression of emotional pain, believing protest to suggest rebellion against God's will, most Moslems will display grief openly, crying and weeping in public.

Mourning usually lasts for 40 days, with the imam reading from the Koran for the first 3 days after the death and then every Friday for the rest of the mourning period. For the first 3 days the bereaved family stay at home and their relatives and friends are duty-bound to visit them, bringing food, comfort and support. The relatives also have a duty to talk about the person who has died and share the loss. During the period of mourning the grave is visited on Fridays (the Islamic holy day) and alms are distributed to the poor. Relatives of the deceased are not supposed to listen to music, watch television or indulge in any other form of entertainment throughout the 40 days. Photographs and television sets are covered with a cloth. These and other rituals are important and great comfort is gained by carrying out as much religious practice as possible.

Hinduism

Hinduism is a very ancient religion with many gods and goddesses who are all believed to be manifestations of the one God. This may often seem confusing to a non-Hindu. It is a religion of many forms with many ways of worship, prayer and meditation. It is also a 'way-of-life', which offers great support and comfort to its believers.

The Hindu design for living suggests that as a person reaches the third and fourth (final) part or stage of their life they should be preparing to sever relationships on earth, so that the spirit may be released to unite with the Supreme Being. These stages of life suggest that there is a time for all things, and the Hindu believes in a return to earth in a better or worse form according to one's Karma. The Karma represents the idea that what the individual does in this world affects what will happen to him in the next. Although Hindus sometimes regard health as a reward for living according to religious and moral laws in a previous life, and therefore regard ill-health as a punishment, most Hindus regard their actual death as insignificant because of their certainty of being with God in the afterlife. Hindu priests or brahmins (who are top of the caste system) will help those who are dying to accept the inevitable and it is important that a brahmin is present, and indeed is fed, as part of the mourning ceremony.

Death is usually accepted without the manifestations of anger which characterise Judaism, Christianity and Islam. As death draws near the dying person is given water from the River Ganges and passages from holy books are read out. After a Hindu dies, non-Hindus must wear gloves if they need to touch the body. The family usually prefer to wash the body and lay it out, covered by a white sheet. Cremation is the rule and should be done on the day of the death. This is impractical in Britain, but in recognition of this rule all bureaucratic procedures should be done as quickly as possible. The ashes are either scattered on the River Ganges, or into a river flowing into the ocean. A ceremony called Sraddha on the 11th day after the death involves certain rites for the dead, usually performed by the eldest son. Relatives, friends and neighbours are all bound to be involved in the showing of respect through this ceremony. Grief is expressed openly with much crying and the consolation and support given to the bereaved is regarded as most important. The 13th day marks the end of official mourning after which men may shave and cut their hair again and may eat non-vegetarian food.

Hindu religious practice varies enormously between different groups but what is common is a shared attitude to human life. This attitude is very different from that in western cultures and it needs to be recognised as such and accepted.

Sikhism

In a sense Sikhism can be seen as an offshoot of Hinduism, since it was started in the early sixteenth century by Guru Nanak and his disciples (Sikh = disciple, follower), who were disaffected Hindus and particularly deplored the caste system. They had no priesthood and emphasised each individual's relationship with God and his search for the virtuous life by doing good in this world. Sikhs have developed a strong community sense and each community runs its own gurdwara. This is the temple as well as a place for hospitality and an advice centre. It is here that the service is usually held after the death. Sikhs hold both to a belief in the value of communal service as part of a commitment to actions in this life, and to a belief in the doctrine of Karma, like the Hindus, where each soul goes through cycles of birth and rebirth, aiming to reach perfection, and be united with God.

Again, the doctrine of reincarnation seems to render Sikhs less frightened of death, unless they feel their next life is likely to be considerably worse than the current one. They do believe in a forgiving God.

When a Sikh is close to death the family pray at the bedside and read from the holy book, Guru Granth Sahib. Once the person has died the family lay out the body and ensure that the five signs of Sikhism are worn. The body is viewed before cremation, which is mandatory, and should be done as soon as possible. It is the custom for the heir (usually the eldest son) to light the funeral pyre. In Britain, pushing the button at the crematorium could be perceived as a poor substitute. After the funeral more prayers are said at the gurdwara and when the whole family returns home for the ten days of mourning, friends and relatives come and visit with comfort and support. After ten days or so of intensive mourning, a special ceremony called Bhog marks the official end of mourning. Obviously some families or individuals may need longer depending on their experiences around the death and any difficulties they may have experienced with the funeral in Britain.

Buddhism

Buddhism is a unique religion, which does not recognise a God as creator and is more of a philosophical system or way of life than a religion. It was started around 500 BC by an Indian prince, Siddhartha Gautama, who became the Buddha after his personal 'enlightenment'. Buddhism teaches that greed, hatred and delusion separate people from the true nature of the world. Buddhists seek morality, wisdom and compassion, culminating in a transformation of consciousness known as 'enlightenment'. This is often associated with an inner 'spaciousness' from which all beings become manifest. Some branches deify certain aspects of this 'spaciousness'.

Buddhism is an open religion and has many forms and 'schools' which co-exist peacefully. All the varieties, however, show a great acceptance of the cycle of life and death. For some Buddhists the moment of death is considered very important. Most Buddhists are likely to want to meditate around the time of death and, although not opposed to pain relief, will wish to be in a state of 'mindfulness'. The period just after death is important too, as consciousness is still departing the body, so it is important not to touch it at this point. The winding sheet for a Buddhist must be without emblems and Buddhists are normally cremated, the ceremony often being conducted by a member of the family.

Non-affiliated groups

For some people in contemporary society the form of the funeral ritual may pose a problem, particularly if they are without religious beliefs and think they have no choice about ritual. If they have made no plan for the funeral they may find themselves with no options other than those proposed by the undertaker. Usually, if no other suggestions are offered, the undertaker will propose a Christian service. It is, however, possible to exercise considerable choice about the form of both the burial and cremation services. Humanists, for instance, have created their own personal rituals for the legally required disposal of their relative's or friend's remains after death.

GENERAL CONSIDERATIONS

Having considered, however briefly, the range of beliefs and rituals in our society it is important to recognise that complex issues of culture and race may arise. In situations where counselling takes place between people of different cultural and racial backgrounds, there are many ways in which the useful effects of counselling may be hindered or even destroyed by a counsellor who is unaware of these complexities. These might include, for example, inappropriate use of language, differences in non-verbal behaviours, prejudicial and racist attitudes, incorrect assumptions and lack of knowledge about the process of cross-cultural counselling.

Considerable debate amongst counsellors in the UK has centred around such issues. One view holds that having the skills and attitudes of a counsellor which would include the attitude of complete acceptance of the client's world view and the ability to empathise with the individual, would be sufficient to work effectively with any client (see chapter 2). Further, any specific knowledge about religious or cultural phenomena which was of significance to the client would be supplied by the client. This view implies that there is no need to learn about cultures other than one's own and that racism just simply would not occur between accepting individuals.

An alternative view is that we are so formed by our race, culture and experience that we simply cannot work effectively with people of different racial origins or cultural or life experiences whatever our theoretical knowledge may be.

A third view increasingly supported in the counselling profession holds that in order to understand relationships between people of different racial or cultural experience and origin and to work effectively with them, a knowledge of the different groups and of the history between the various groups is essential. However, this knowledge must be underpinned by an understanding of racism and of how contemporary society works in relation to race, the exercise of power and the effects of discrimination. Furthermore counsellors require a personal awareness of where they stand in relation to these issues and of when and in what ways these issues may influence and need to be addressed in the counselling process.

At the beginning of this chapter we recognised some common human needs which may underlie the variety of cultural patterns on which we then focused. It may be useful, therefore, to end this chapter by recognising a common twentieth-century struggle succinctly expressed by the writer, psychoanalyst and sociologist Erich Fromm (1978), when he states: 'There is only one way – taught by the Buddha, by Jesus, by the Stoics, by Master Eckhart – to truly overcome the fear of dying, and that is by not hanging on to life, not experiencing life as a possession. . . . The fear then is not of dying, but of losing what I have; the fear of losing my body, my ego, my possessions, and my identity; the fear of facing the abyss of non-identity, of "being lost".'

SUMMARY

1 While the patterns of responses in different cultures to death and mourning vary enormously, there are three elements common to virtually all cultures; these relate to the changing relationships with the dead person, to the allocation of blame and expression of anger and to the length of mourning.
2 Cultural rituals are helpful in guiding us through the transition of grief and in managing the often extreme emotions of anger, uncertainty and fear evoked by the death. Emotional connections to a cultural or social group enable individuals to use these rituals more effectively.
3 Knowledge of beliefs about death and the afterlife and about mourning practices in different religious and cultural groups is essential in our multi-ethnic and multi-belief society.
4 Awareness of racism in society and in ourselves can also enable us to work more sensitively with people of ethnic origins different from our own.

7

CHILDREN'S GRIEF

In chapter 1 we saw how, after the separation of birth, a baby is 'grappling' with attachment and separation from its earliest days. We also saw how children who were separated from their parents by going to hospital, for instance, protested angrily and then despaired. The angry protest went on to alternate with despair as long as hope for reattachment could be maintained. If, however, a child reached a period of detachment then it was difficult for her to reattach either to the old attachment figure or to a new caretaker. These studies help us to get some idea of the immensity of children's grief when they are separated from their parents or caretakers.

We also saw in chapter 5 how prevalent the denial of death is in our culture in the twentieth century. Adults introduce this process of embarrassed denial early in a child's life. In modern western societies children are rarely given much information about death. Where the topic cannot be avoided it is often treated in a vague or unrealistic manner. What sense can a child make of a remark such as 'Grandad's gone on a journey', when the adult actually means that Grandad has died? This is one form of denial.

Another form of denial may find expression through an apparently protective act. For instance we often go to enormous lengths to 'protect' children from the sight of a dead body. They may also be 'protected' from going to a funeral. This 'protection' starts early in a child's life and it may be that the piercing cry of the infant re-awakens in us, as adults, the painful experience of our early childhood losses. We avoid the revival of these excruciating feelings by quietening or diverting the child and denying the hurt of her loss. The effect of the intensity of the child's feelings on adults' experience can help us to understand how it is that children's grief is so ignored. How often do we hear 'Oh, but he's too young to understand' or 'She can't be missing her Dad, he left us after all' or 'Isn't she good? We've had no tears at all'? The following story illustrates this point.

Some years ago now, a friend, Patricia, who came for coffee with her 5-year-old son, arrived hiding her distress. As soon as the children had gone out to play she told me that Sam had died that night. 'How awful', I said, 'but who is Sam?' 'Sam is Pete's guinea-pig and this will break his heart, how can I tell him? My sister will get us a new guinea-pig by tomorrow. But how can I spare him the pain? I can at least tell him that Sam is in heaven, can't I?' 'Is that what you truly believe?' – 'Oh don't be silly, of course I don't, but how can I make it less painful for him?' 'Perhaps you can't. Perhaps you would be unwise to. Perhaps Pete has a right to his feelings and his grief over Sam's death.' 'But he's only a child, how can he understand what death means?' 'Perhaps this is the way he can find out what death means.' Patricia and I argued for a bit until I think she began to realise that Pete would actually endure Sam's death better if she allowed him to feel his feelings and experience his loss.

In our efforts to protect children from pain we may deprive them of their own best means of managing pain and overcoming the effects of loss. Children use such life events as the death of a guinea-pig to help them understand death and mortality. If their feelings in relation to such losses can be validated and understood this will help them to recognise and deal with the possible griefs of childhood.

Perhaps one of the commonest griefs of childhood in Britain today is the circumstantial loss of a parent through separation and divorce. Divorce is a difficult process for all participants. The parents may be so caught up in their feelings of hurt and anger that the child's pain and confusion goes unrecognised. Other circumstantial losses which some children experience are going into foster care; changing foster-parents; being adopted; moving house or school; failure at school; loss of health through accident or illness; loss of trust of adults owing to physical or sexual abuse; and, of course, the loss of a parent through death. In many of these circumstances the children's grief is simply disregarded by encouraging them to think only of the gain. All too often a child is told, when one of her parents remarries, 'Aren't you lucky! You now have brothers and sisters.' In this there is no recognition of the child's loss of intimacy with her own parent who has remarried.

It is, of course, particularly difficult for children at the time when the grief goes unrecognised, but the consequences in adult life are profound. We know from working with adults how often their difficulties stem from unacknowledged losses in childhood. A study of depressed women in Camberwell (Brown and Harris, 1978) showed that one of four vulnerability factors, which predisposed women to suffer from depression, was the loss of their mothers before the age of 11. This childhood loss had clearly contributed to these women's depression. Since unrecognised childhood losses can affect adult life in this way, it is useful to consider the experience of grief at the different stages of children's development.

0-2 YEARS

Children's understanding of loss and death changes as they grow and develop. For the baby under 6 months we can assume that as the attachment intensifies so the experience of separation intensifies, and this loss will be experienced as if it were a death. Should the mother die this will be experienced exactly as if she had gone away and the quality of substitute care will be enormously important.

For the older infant between 6 months and 2 years we can see the beginnings of grief and mourning in a child's behaviour. She will search for her mother, call out for her and ask for her, even though she has no concept of 'death' as such. The notion of 'finality' will come only slowly. She will initially protest, then feel despair and gradually detach. She will be loath to let other attachment figures out of her sight. Her sadness will be almost palpable and it is at this stage that denial of the child's grief may be most intense. Few children in this age group will have conscious memories of parents who have died. When they are older this frequently results in fantasies of a perfect parent. Thus, when told off by their mother, for instance, they will fantasise that their dead daddy 'would not have been nasty' to them. If this fantasy remains unrecognised it can cause considerable problems for the surviving parent and step-parent should remarriage occur.

2-5 YEARS

There are few systematic studies of grief and mourning in early childhood. In one study by Rochlin (1967) of children in the 3–5 age group, he found that they thought a lot about death, were aware that it represented the end of vital functions and were interested in the causality of death. This is the age when children are most likely to ask openly about death and tend to drag home such delights as dead seagulls! Yet for all the child at this age may be the 'little scientist', she is also highly susceptible to fantasies. Bowlby (1979) points out that for these young children fantasies about death may be reinforced by parental comments before the death such as 'You'll be the death of me'. A child is also likely to be very confused by explanations of death such as 'like going to sleep' or 'not waking up again'. It would be hardly surprising in these circumstances if a child were to become reluctant to go to bed. She may well be associating going to sleep with becoming like the dead seagull. Although she may have some vague concept of death, she may not be able to associate this 'scientific' concept with the actual experience of loss through death, should she be bereaved at this time. Her feelings are likely to be expressed very directly and there is less control or constraint of feelings. She also struggles to find words to fit feelings and will be enormously helped when adults can give her clear words and concepts. The child needs to know as clearly as possible what it is that has happened to cause her loss. She will probably need to ask again and again as she grapples with these difficult ideas. Her relationship with the adults around will affect how she manages her grief and mourning. She may find it difficult to put her feelings and memories into words, just when the adults find her reminders of the death, and her painful mourning unbearable for them. As they struggle with their own feelings they may not be able to empathise with her feelings and will therefore fail to understand her.

However, if the adult can listen she will hear the child's message behind the words. You will remember Anne's story (chapter 3). Just as she was wondering how on earth to manage her own feelings and tell Michael about his father's death, Michael helped make the link.

Anne's 2-year-old son Michael had been staying with grandparents over the last couple of days of James's life to enable her to be with James and attend to baby Pete's needs. When Michael returned the day after James's death he didn't go and look for him which rather surprised Anne and she, still pretty numb, didn't quite know what to do or say. After lunch Michael helped her:

Anne: Would you like a Polo, Michael?
Michael: These are Daddy's Polos.
Anne: That's right, they were Daddy's Polos. But Daddy won't be needing them any more, because Daddy's not here now.

Michael then pensively ate the Polo, had a good cuddle with Anne and returned to playing with his favourite cuddly toy. That was probably enough information for that day but there were many fears, nightmares and strong feelings to be worked through before Michael could be said to have resolved his grief.

5–8 YEARS

A child in the 5–8 age-group is developing fast and beginning to get a sense of the idea of the 'future'. She can therefore begin to understand ideas such as 'Daddy won't be living with us *any more*' or 'Grandad is dead and we won't *ever* see him *again*'. At this stage too the child is developing the capacity to feel guilt but not able to understand the difference between feelings and acts. Thus the child's growing understanding of her own actions will often lead her to think she actually caused the loss herself, e.g. 'it was because I got cross with Grandad that he died' or 'I cried until I was allowed to sit next to Mummy at tea and not Daddy and that's why Daddy's left us'.

Further, children often do not make a distinction between thought and action. They can believe that when they are so angry that they wished someone dead, their thoughts actually killed the dead person. To counteract this tendency children need to be listened to and their fantasies and 'magical thinking' explored, so that they can discover that they were not the cause of the death, the departure or the abuse. Children of this age-group will quickly deny their own feelings, either when feelings are difficult for them to handle themselves, or when they sense that an adult cannot manage the feelings. Children will actually protect an adult in this way, particularly in the case of abuse, but suffer in the process by carrying

---

Exercise 7.1 Example of a grieving child

Paul was almost 7 when his father, Thomas, was killed in a car accident (Exercise 8.1). The accident happened after Paul went to bed and he only knew next morning. He cried for a few minutes but when encouraged to go to school he went easily. From then on he never cried about his father and rarely talked about him. He always seemed exceptionally good and well behaved. However, the family did notice that from about the time of his father's death he was really clinging with his mother, Susan. Whenever she went out in the evening he would say nothing but she would see his little face, with tears streaming down, glued to the window. This became progressively worse as did bed-wetting. His teacher noticed that he frequently did not know that she had spoken to him.

About 2 years later Susan was feeling really anxious about 9-year-old Paul, particularly when she found her favourite scarf, which she wore a lot, hidden in Paul's bedroom. It had been missing some time and Paul had been asked more than once if he had seen it. He hadn't. When she found it, Paul still said he didn't know the scarf was in his room. Susan decided at this point to seek help. In talking she realised that Paul needed help with grieving and that he was showing signs of grief in more ways than she had realised.

What signs of grief can you find?

---

on as if nothing had happened. Usually, however, the sensitive observer can see the signs of grief in the hurt child.

In the story of Paul's bereavement in Exercise 7.1 we see how his grief was not recognised and his frightening feelings went underground. He then had to try to express his grief indirectly through his behaviour. This behaviour was trying to express what could not be said in words.

You will have noticed some signs of grief in Paul in Exercise 7.1. It was difficult for Susan to notice these at the time as she was, naturally enough, preoccupied with her own grief. In such circumstances adults will often be struggling with their own grief, so that listening to and understanding the children can be very difficult. This leaves the children isolated and much in need of external support. We turn now to look at how Susan came to recognise and work with Paul's grief.

Encouraged by a listener, Val, Susan started talking to Paul about Thomas. Gradually Paul told Susan that Thomas had been really cross with him just before he left for a meeting on the night he died. He had sent Paul to bed and Paul had been very angry with Thomas. Susan also remembered the incident.

Val suggested to Susan that maybe Paul had been so angry with his father that night that he had wished him dead. Paul found it very hard to tell Susan that this was so, but then he blurted out 'It's all my fault, I killed him.' Susan then took Paul on her knee and told him that she understood his reasoning, but that it was not actually true that he had killed his father. She needed to tell him this several times more before he could really believe it. Gradually his clinging behaviour stopped.

Talking with Val, Susan reflected that there were many ways in which Paul was stuck as a '7 year old'. When Susan asked Paul if he felt as though he was still 7, he said 'Yes, that's how Daddy remembers me.'

In this example we have thought about the possible meaning of some signs of grief. In Paul's case, his going back or regression to a '7 year old' seemed to be his way of trying to express his need to deal with something which happened when he was 'aged 7'. He may also have feared that, were he to grow up and become a real 9 year old, he would be unrecognisable to Thomas. It was almost as if he retained a hope that by remaining age 7 his father would recognise him if he returned from the dead. His clinging behaviour was his way of saying to Susan 'Please don't go in case my angry feelings kill you as well as Daddy.' His taking the scarf may have been his way of saying 'If I express my badness this way then perhaps I won't have to kill you' and perhaps also 'The scarf means I do have a bit of you, if and when you do die.' Once Susan was able to begin to unravel his fears, his fantasies and behaviour could be understood and his grief then expressed more appropriately.

Table 7.1 summarises the behavioural messages Paul used to express his grief indirectly, and the help that enabled him to understand and express his feelings more directly. This list tells us something about the way Paul expressed his grief. Other children will use different ways to express their grief. Some of these, such as overassiduousness at school, overcleanliness and overtidiness are sometimes encouraged by overwrought parents and not recognised as part of a grieving pattern. Other, more obvious signs such as soiling, school avoidance, nightmares, accident-proneness, breaking up friendships, taking other people's possessions, may be very trying for the other grieving siblings and parent. The signs of grief outlined above refer to children bereaved by the death of a parent, but children grieving in a divorcing family will behave in similar ways (Burgoyne, 1984; Clulow and Mattinson, 1989). We consider other ways of helping such children in chapter 11.

Table 7.1 Some signs of grieving in a child

Signs of Paul's grief	Help required
1 Overdependence on living parent. Frightened and clinging behaviour. Difficulty with every separation.	Recognition and understanding of Paul's feelings of fear about losing the other parent. Recognition of his fear of Susan's death or disappearance, perhaps as a 'result' of his angry feelings.
2 Day-dreaming	Recognition of Paul's difficulty in facing reality and the need to escape, possibly into a fantasy world. This world might be explored.
3 Wetting	Understanding of Paul's need to become a 'little boy again'. Helping him to express his need for caring in a more appropriate way.
4 Symbolic stealing and 'forgetting'	Recognition of the meaning to Paul of his taking 'something of Susan', enabling him to express his fear of losing her.
5 Excessive fear and compliant behaviour becoming 'bad behaviour'	Recognition of Paul's fear of being punished again. Once this fear lifts there is sometimes a period of difficult behaviour, which may usefully express the angry feelings which went underground.

8–12 YEARS

Magical thinking is beginning to diminish in the 8–12-year-old child as she understands and is more oriented towards the future. Thus she has the cognitive ability to realise what the loss will mean to her. The death of, or separation from, a parent threatens her and can reawaken feelings of childishness and helplessness. She may show outwardly coping behaviour but may be denying the feelings inside, not resolving the loss and thus delaying the grieving process.

In Geoff's story (chapter 3) we have in Christine's behaviour a typical example of this coping behaviour. On the morning of her mother's sudden death, she remembered that it was the school photograph that day and that she had to wash her hair. Outwardly she coped beautifully. It was only in her late teens that Christine was able to experience deeply the pain of grief about her mother's tragic death. A child in this age group may also become involved in symbolic behaviour and, for instance, become obsessed by the dead parent's possessions. This is a way of trying to express a longing to hold on to and continue the lost relationship as it was.

The dawning sexuality of this pubescent period, together with growing sexual identity, may complicate relationships with parents, sometimes leading to a pulling away from one parent and an increased identity with the other. The 8–12 year old usually 'identifies' increasingly with the parent of the same sex and will be particularly affected if that parent dies or leaves. When this grief is particularly difficult to express it may be shown indirectly through behaviour patterns not unlike those outlined for Paul in Table 7.1.

It is at this stage of development too that children come to recognise the possibility of their own deaths. This identification with death may make the subject particularly frightening for them. This probably intensifies the tendency towards denial, and it may be necessary to be quite firm with this age group to give them the opportunity to share their longing, their feelings and their memories with us. When they do trust us they will usually respond to this kind of encouragement. As they begin to share their memories and feelings, their behaviour usually becomes understandable as a sign of grief.

ADOLESCENCE

Adolescence itself is a period of loss as well as gain. For the passing of childhood and separation from the first family needs to be mourned, just as much as the new sexual possibilities and growing independence of adolescence need to be welcomed. There is much upheaval during the period of adolescence and relationships with peers, siblings and parents pass through many phases as the young person moves towards separation and reorganisation. An additional separation task such as the death or loss of a parent through divorce coming at this time is particularly challenging, especially in early adolescence when self-confidence may be lowest.

Adolescents' mourning process for the death or loss of a parent, sibling or friend follows the usual pattern and if the powerful feelings and the mood swings can be expressed and understood it will take its natural course. When adolescents identify very closely with a lost person they may take on their mannerisms, behaviours and values. Identification with a more 'adult' person is a natural aspect of adolescence. It is usually short-lived, and may change from week to week (changing allegiances to pop-stars, for instance). If, however, this 'overidentification' with the lost person continues and does not shift, then adolescents may need help to get in touch with their anger with the lost person for 'deserting' or 'abandoning' them at this important stage. With this help they may then begin to let go of the lost person and be able to get on with their own developmental tasks. This may include some depressed and aggressive feelings as adolescents begin to experience the pain of the loss and recognise the need to find a new identity without the lost person. This seems to be particularly true for boys who have lost a father (Van Eerdewegh et al., 1982).

Our own experience of adolescent girls is that they too usually have periods of depression in response to loss. Another way in which adolescent girls often try to manage a difficult loss is to deny the grief and become 'the little caretaker'. This pseudo-adult, 'bossy' and powerfully controlling behaviour then masks the girl's own need for comfort. This role also serves to protect her from feeling the pain and emptiness which the loss has caused.

In Geoff's story his eldest daughter Julie, who was 12 when her mother died so suddenly, seemed to slip almost effortlessly into the 'little mother' role. It was she who stayed off school the following day to 'help with the other two'. It was she who accompanied father to work before going to the coroner's office and the doctors. It was she who discussed with her father whether they felt strong enough to read the letters that day. In some sense she 'couldn't be a child' any more for there was no mother and she 'managed' this by becoming a 'little mother' herself. But as others worked through events and feelings, she needed to maintain her role and tried to control everyone by behaving in a 'bossy' and controlling manner. This meant that although people said, 'Isn't she wonderful', Julie was not getting the comfort she needed and her feelings of anger and sadness were increasingly denied. It was many months before Julie's increasingly angry and controlling outbursts were recognised as her attempt to deny her grief rather than experience the pain of her great loss. Once she could risk recognising her own pain she swung back to being a 'very little girl' refusing all age-appropriate responsibility. This may have been her way of trying to get the comfort she had refused before. Eventually she was able to be her own 'real age', appropriately caring for others and being cared for herself.

Late-adolescent girls may try to 'fill the gap' left by the loss of someone important to them by becoming pregnant. If the pregnancy leads to abortion or miscarriage, then the grief over the lost child, who might have filled the gap, is likely to be intense. However, it often goes unrecognised, with people suggesting that the abortion or miscarriage was 'for the best'. If the child is born, the young mother may find enormous difficulty in letting the child find its own identity, perhaps because the baby is treated as if it were the lost person.

With children of any age who have been sexually abused, the loss of innocence is a severe wound which usually remains deep inside and unrecognised because of the pressures towards secrecy. Often these wounds remain secret into adulthood, only emerging if the person is lucky and forms a loving relationship. If such a relationship cannot be established then the wound may go unrecognised for decades. The inappropriate guilt and appropriate anger of those who have been sexually abused will be considered, albeit rather briefly, in chapter 12.

In this chapter we have seen that children do indeed grieve but frequently mask their grief. When children are encouraged to express their true feelings then they can be helped. The following quotation from Beverley Raphael (1984) illustrates just such an interaction.

> Jessica was 5. She showed her mother the picture she had painted. There were black clouds, dark trees and large red splashes.
> 'My,' said her mother. 'Tell me all about this, Jess.' Jessica pointed to the red splashes. 'That's blood,' she said. 'And these are clouds.' 'Oh,' said her mother. 'See,' said Jessica, 'the trees are very sad. The clouds are black. They are sad too.' 'Why are they sad?' asked her mother. 'They are sad because their Daddy has died,' said Jessica, the tears slowly running down her cheeks. 'Sad like us since Daddy died,' said her mother and held her closely, and they wept.
>
> (Beverley Raphael: 138)

In families which have developed their relationships with openness and shared feelings, a child can usually express her grief and can receive comfort. She is, of course, hurt by the loss but there will be healing and she will not fear life because of it. Families who find difficulty in expressing feelings openly will often need help with grief. We will look at some practical examples of working with grieving children in chapter 11.

SUMMARY

1 Children do grieve if adults recognise this and allow them to do so.

2 Frequently adults deny children's grief, in the guise of 'protecting' the children.
3 Children frequently mask their grief.
4 Circumstantial losses which children experience are: being fostered or adopted; divorce of parent; moving house, community or school; failure at school; loss of health; disability, etc.
5 The experience of grief for children has specific features linked to their emotional development.
6 Children often express their grief indirectly through altered behaviour.
7 Sexually abused children can carry a deep wound of loss into early and sometimes late adult life.

8

PERSONAL AND FAMILY
EXPERIENCES OF LOSS

Up to this point we have looked at bereavement largely through the eyes of the researcher and through our own personal experiences. As loss counsellors we need to be able to apply this knowledge to bereaved people and we also need to know whether what has been said about bereavement is true for other losses. If that is indeed the case, then we can extrapolate from bereavement to other losses, whether natural or circumstantial.

The aims of this chapter are twofold: to enable you to apply knowledge about bereavement to specific families and situations, including your own, and to see whether the response to loss has similarities to bereavement. In thinking about how bereavement will affect a particular family we have to look at the individuals who are bereaved, their family network and their past history. An example of such a family is given through the family tree outlined in Table 8.1 on page 69.

Introducing you to so many people in this family at this stage may seem rather unnecessary. Yet any one loss within a family will undoubtedly affect others, particularly those who themselves are still in the process of their own grief. Grief has been called a social process and this is nowhere more true than within the wider family circle. For the ways of handling grief, or indeed denial of grief, tend to be reflected or repeated from one generation to the next. It is often the case that the more we can understand the feelings, relationships and griefs in ourselves and our own generation, the more we can understand those of past as well as future generations.

Members of the family represented in Table 8.1 have experienced loss through death, emigration, divorce, handicap and miscarriage. No doubt other losses such as going to school, moving house and losing jobs have also happened to them. In Exercise 8.1 (page 70) we invite you to think about this extended family, in particular about Susan and Thomas and their family.

In thinking about each member of the family, consider both the external determining circumstances surrounding them and their particular personal history (see chapter 4). This will give you ideas about how each individual's grief might be expressed, whether the grief process could become blocked and the likelihood of their needing extra support.

Table 8.1 Family tree

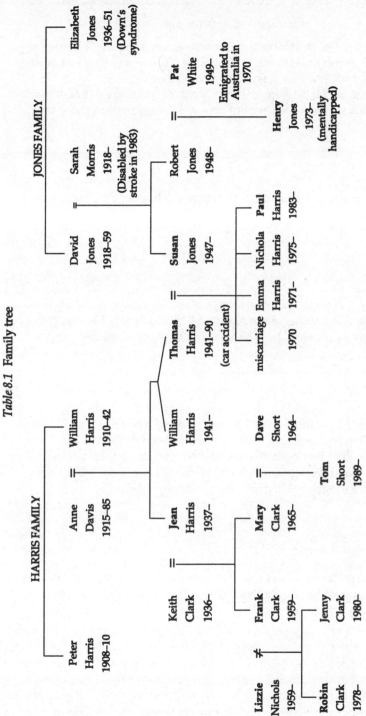

Note. Names in bold refer to the people we have used to illustrate points in the text.

Exercise 8.1 Use of the family tree

1 **Consider Susan Harris in 1990 when her husband Thomas was killed in a car accident. At that time Emma was away at college and Nichola and Paul were at school locally.**
   a) Think about the support sources which might exist for Susan. The families' experience of loss will be particularly relevant.

   b) What about the position of William, Thomas's identical twin brother?

   c) Paul's 7th birthday was 5 days after Thomas's death. Should Susan let Paul have the planned birthday party? When should Thomas's funeral be? Does Paul have special needs?

   d) How might the death of Susan's father when she was 12 affect the current grieving? Susan had one bout of depression soon after Paul was born. Though recovered, might this previous postnatal depression be a significant factor now? Might her miscarriage in 1970 affect her grieving now?

2 **Consider Robert Jones and Patricia White, now in Australia.**
   a) What position might they have found themselves in when Henry was born?

Exercise 8.1 (continued)

b) How might they have been affected by Thomas's death?

3 In what ways might the Welsh origins of the Jones family affect the rituals of grief?

4 Have these families experienced exceptional numbers of losses?

5 There are many other losses in this family tree. You might like to focus on other members and, given the information you have, consider what determinants would affect each of their losses.

The family tree is one way of looking at what factors affect grieving throughout a whole family. By drawing a lifeline (as in Table 8.2, page 72) for a particular member of a family, we can highlight all the losses in one individual's life and focus in on their 'loss-history' more clearly.

Let us try to illustrate this by looking in more detail at Jean Clark, Tom's grandmother. Jean, aged 55, has just had an accident and this loss now has been influenced in various ways by her earlier experiences. We can use her lifeline to focus on important events in the past, which may be influencing present circumstances.

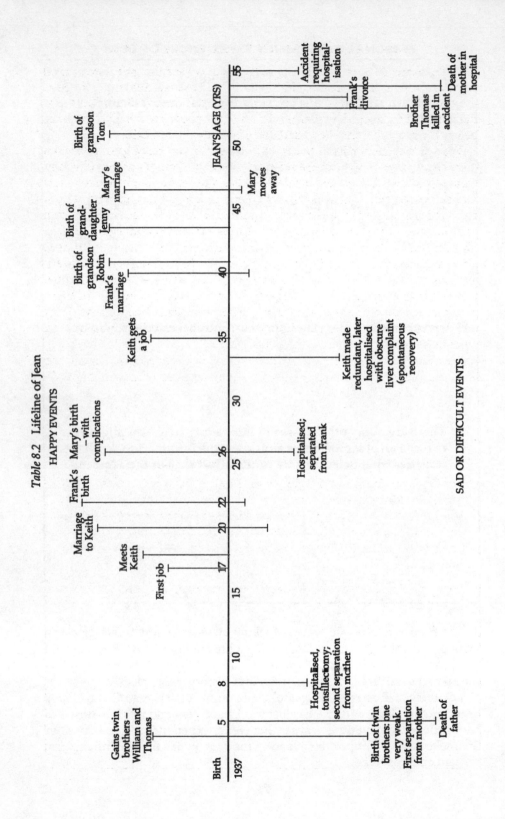

Table 8.2 Lifeline of Jean

HAPPY EVENTS

Gains twin brothers – William and Thomas

First job

Meets Keith

Marriage to Keith

Frank's birth

Mary's birth – with complications

Keith gets a job

Birth of grandson Robin

Frank's marriage

Birth of grand-daughter Jenny

Mary's marriage

Birth of grandson Tom

Accident requiring hospital-isation

JEAN'S AGE (YRS)

Birth   1937   5   8   10   15   17   20   22   25   26   30   35   40   45   50   55

Birth of twin brothers: one very weak. First separation from mother

Death of father

Hospitalised, tonsillectomy; second separation from mother

Hospitalised; separated from Frank

Keith made redundant, later hospitalised with obscure liver complaint (spontaneous recovery)

Mary moves away

Frank's divorce

Brother Thomas killed in accident

Death of mother in hospital

SAD OR DIFFICULT EVENTS

In the example of Jean's lifeline in Table 8.2 we see that she has marked some of the events in her life. She has indicated the relative importance of the event by the length of the line away from the central lifeline and also the meaning by deciding whether the line goes above for a happy event or below the central lifeline for a sad or difficult event, or both.

We see that the births of her two children and her three grandchildren were happy events for Jean. Separations from her mother and her children were sad or difficult events; the death of her mother being particularly sad for her. Some events, such as the birth of her twin brothers, have been both gain and loss simultaneously. She experienced her marriage mainly as a gain, but she was also aware of the loss of freedom which marriage signified for her. The birth of her daughter Mary, and later the marriage of Frank, also contained these mixed elements. We notice in comparing Jean's various losses that, for her, many of these were linked with periods in hospital. When Jean is hospitalised it is possible that any one, or indeed all, of these previous experiences may be influencing the way she is feeling now. A lot will depend on how her earlier losses were experienced at the time and on what these previous losses still mean for her.

Jean has a life story with losses, as do we all, but she will also experience multiple losses when she goes into hospital. The story of Jean's hospitalisation is told in Exercise 8.2.

Exercise 8.2 Multiple losses

Tom's Gran, Jean, and her husband Keith live 40 miles from their daughter, Mary, and her family, and 200 miles from their son, Frank, and his family. She has a job and she and Keith have enjoyed holidays and outings since the children left home. She was recently knocked down and seriously injured by a drunken driver and is now in hospital.

Can you list some of the losses which Jean experienced while in hospital?

Some of the losses and changes Jean is likely to have experienced are loss of freedom, loss of health, loss of safety, loss of sexual intimacy, loss of expectations (she may well not be able to walk for some time), loss of hobbies, loss of comfort, temporary loss of job and associated interests, loss of routine, etc. These multiple losses can have profound effects on people. For some the only way to cope with being looked after is to become compliant and in some ways childlike if not childish. Others seem to find their greatest maturity at such times of crisis. Studying the lifeline of Jean's loss-history can help us to understand more about her likely responses to the multiple losses she experienced in hospital.

DRAWING YOUR OWN LIFELINE

Jean's lifeline in Table 8.2 shows her life-history and the weight she gave to the losses and gains associated with various events in her life. In Exercise 8.3 we give you the opportunity to look at your own life history in the same way.

As you look at your lifeline now, think about any picture or pattern of feelings which emerges and take time to reflect on that. You might also like to think about whether some events have left you with unresolved or ambivalent feelings and thoughts. Also take time to reflect on your own personal history. The counselling attitudes of acceptance, congruence and empathy are firmly based in self-knowledge and counsellors need to be aware of their own life history, in particular their own feelings and vulnerabilities. Many people find it difficult to share their own personal feelings, and yet in a counselling relationship it is what we expect others to do. It would, therefore, be important for you to share some of the feelings you know to be associated with events in your life, with someone else, preferably someone you do not know too well. This will give you the chance to experience what it is like to share your own personal feelings with a near stranger. It will also give you the opportunity to discover more about your feelings in relationship to past losses.

Exercise 8.3 Your lifeline

Using Jean's lifeline (Table 8.2) as an example, create your own personal lifeline from the line printed below.* Mark off your current age and put a cross on the line at each age that a significant event occurred in your life. (These might be events such as the birth of a brother or sister, leaving home, marriage, death of someone special, birth of children, job loss, etc.) Then for each event draw a vertical line either above or below the central (horizontal) line, or indeed both above and below. Lines above the central line indicate a happy event and below the central line a sad or difficult event. Some events may be both sad and happy. Indicate the relative importance of the event for you by the length of the vertical line.

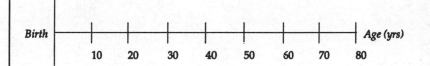

Once you have completed your lifeline as indicated, go back in your memory to these events and see if you can remember the feelings associated with the events or the period of the events. As you remember the feelings write them down.

*You can, of course, create your own size of lifeline on a separate sheet.

Table 8.3 summarises the feelings of other people who have used a lifeline to discover the feelings they had which were associated with losses in their lives.

Table 8.3 Feelings associated with loss

Shock	Guilt	Hopelessness
Searching	Fear	Helplessness
Disbelief	Ambivalence	Anxiety
Anger	Isolation	Loneliness
Hate	Frustration	Acceptance
Bitterness	Despair	

Compare your feelings associated with the losses in your life (Exercise 8.3) with those of others. It is likely that many of your feelings will be similar to those in Table 8.3 of others experiencing a loss. If this is the case it will make sense to you that when loss occurs certain feelings can be expected. These feelings will vary in intensity for different people at different times but they are the natural response to loss and an inevitable part of being human.

If you then compare the feelings from Table 8.3 with a child's response to a sudden long loss as summarised in Table 1.1, you will notice similarities. If you then compare these two tables with the phases of mourning and associated feelings outlined in Table 3.2 you will be able to make further links.

We have tried to simplify these three patterns and brought them together in Table 8.4 to show how they interconnect.

We have also indicated how the feelings associated with adult loss link in an overlapping pattern with Parkes's phases of mourning and feelings associated with grief. From these links we can conclude, first, that the response to bereavement is a specific and a particularly intense example of the generalised response of human beings to loss. Second, bereavement fits into a well-established pattern of response to loss. We have outlined the ways in which external and internal factors can affect the response to bereavement. Such factors will also affect other losses, whether natural or circumstantial.

As loss counsellors it is important that we know about loss in all its ramifications. It is equally important to know our own pattern of grieving and be aware of our own personal loss history, for this will markedly affect how we grieve and how we listen to others' grief. If there are feelings which we as counsellors have never expressed or perhaps do not even feel, then it is unlikely that we will be able to empathise with these feelings in others and we will almost certainly inhibit their expression.

Table 8.4 Comparison between loss reaction in adults and young children

Phases of mourning (C. M. Parkes) (Table 3.2)	Adult loss (your feelings) (Table 8.3)	Childhood loss	
		(Tom's feelings) (Table 1.1)	(Children's attitudes) (Table 1.1)
NUMBNESS	Shock	Shock and	Disbelief in loss
	Disbelief	Anger	(Still hope of recovery of lost person)
YEARNING	Searching	Angry longing	
	Frustration Anger		
	Loneliness	Despair	Belief in loss
	Hate Love		
DISORGANISATION and DESPAIR	Ambivalence	Hopelessness	(No hope of recovery of lost person)
	Guilt		
	Bitterness Isolation		
	Fear	Emptiness	
	Anxiety		
	Despair		Denial of needs
	Hopelessness	Ultimate	
	Helplessness	despair	
REORGANISATION	Acceptance	Reattachment	
	Relief		

SUMMARY

1 Drawing a family tree can help us become more aware of the range of losses affecting a family, of the different ways in which different members are affected and of the interconnectedness of different losses.

2 Within any single loss, multiple losses occur and these are in turn affected by that person's loss history.

3 Drawing our own life-line can help us focus on gains and losses in our lives and on the feelings associated with these events.

4 Certain feelings can be expected in response to all losses including bereavement and childhood separations. The way in which these feelings are experienced and managed is affected by personal loss history.

5 As loss counsellors it is important to know these feelings and their history in ourselves so that we can empathise with those feelings and experiences in others.

Section III

WORKING WITH THE GRIEVING

9

BASIC LOSS COUNSELLING SKILLS

'Give sorrow words'

We have now looked at different aspects of loss and bereavement. In the preceding section we focused on research into bereavement and also experiences of bereavement which can bring us insights about human loss in general. Recognition of loss in our own lives (Exercise 8.3) and the feelings associated with these losses enables us to accept and listen to those who have recently suffered a loss. Therefore when using counselling skills as counsellors we can listen more effectively because we draw on our knowledge of ourselves and the naturalness of our own mourning process. We also have a confidence in the function of grieving and are not surprised that any one loss is experienced as multiple losses or that it evokes feelings from previous losses. Rather like the anthropologists mentioned in chapter 6 our role is to observe, accept and value the experiences of others, trying to understand this experience at many levels yet without wishing to change it in any way.

The particular attitudes of care, nurture and non-judgemental acceptance mentioned in chapter 2 enable others to talk. They can also enable people to stop fearing and condemning their own feelings, to accept their loss and experience their grief to the full.

Attitudes alone are not enough. They have to be conveyed through responses. Responding skills need to be recognised, separated out and learnt. As these learnt skills become integrated into the flow of the relationship, they become counselling.

The difficulty of learning how to integrate skills into a relationship has many parallels with learning how to ride a bicycle, where the mechanics of learning to ride are like the skills, and the balance is like the attitudes. At first you need someone to hold on to the saddle and help you keep your balance as you struggle with the mechanics of keeping the pedals going round; learning you cannot freewheel going uphill; remembering to look ahead and not down at the wheel; thinking about which gear is which and which brake to use; remembering to look behind and give signals. As you begin to get your balance and go off on your own you start to forget about the mechanics, and miss a corner or a gear, or don't brake in time and may

81

even fall off. But, gradually, with practice, your sense of balance grows, you begin to integrate the separate tasks into your overall behaviour, and you discover you're actually riding a bike. Yet, however many skills you possess, if you do not have balance you cannot ride. So with counselling, the skills need to be learned for themselves; but without the necessary attitudes it is not counselling.

In a book of this size we can only provide a brief introduction to skills and attitudes. It is, of course, in the practice of skills in a real relationship that you learn how to use them. But to aid this transition from the written word to the relationship 'out there' we have designed some exercises to be done on your own and, wherever possible, subsequently discussed with a friend or fellow counsellor. On a loss counselling training course these exercises can be adapted by the trainer for skills training work (see chapter 16). In the design of some of these initial exercises we have drawn on ideas from Mearns and Thorne (1988) and also from the Truax and Carkhuff (1967) study we mentioned in chapter 2.

For some of these exercises we have introduced the word 'client'. While we are well aware that the listener may not call themselves a counsellor, nor the grievers necessarily define themselves as 'clients'; none the less we have used the terms counsellor and client in most instances as a kind of shorthand to avoid confusion. The examples are, of course, enormously simplified and assume that the external determinants and internal factors are such that the grief is relatively uncomplicated and that this level of counselling is appropriate. Advanced skills for working with more complicated grief are outlined in chapter 13.

Although only basic skills will actually be discussed in this chapter, in Table 9.1 we have summarised the most important skills for loss counselling and indicated the chapters in which they are considered.

Table 9.1   Skills necessary for loss counselling

Basic skills (chapter 9)	A	Active Listening and Distractions from Listening
	B	Reflecting Experience and Feelings
	C	Reflecting with Deeper Empathy
Further skills (chapter 10)	D	Setting Limits or Boundaries
		a) Beginnings – sessions and relationships
		b) Endings – sessions and relationships
	E	Clarification: Hallucinations, Behaviour, Dreams, Beliefs and Repetitive Thoughts or Images
Working with children (chapter 11)	F	Immediacy about Information and Feelings
	G	a) When Feelings Get 'Lost'
		b) When Information is Lacking
Advanced skills (chapter 13)	H	Working with Guilt and Anger in Complicated Grief; Different Patterns and Dilemmas
Assessment and referral (chapter 14)	I	Assessment Skills
	J	Referral Skills

We have divided them into three levels to indicate that the further and advanced skills cannot be practised without a solid grounding in the basic skills. When the skills are integrated in practice this rather artificial division disappears.

ACTIVE LISTENING AND DISTRACTIONS

This skill is not so much a skill of doing as a skill of being. When humans are faced with a crisis, the urge-to-do can be extraordinarily powerful. Being with a person who is expressing strong feelings can sometimes feel like a crisis and the 'urge-to-do' can tempt us into rushing to 'make it better' with a platitude or other unhelpful response. But it is, of course, not action but reception which comforts. It is a counsellor's task to help a client give words to his sorrow.

It is not easy to find the words to express grief and the listener can easily react to her own anxiety, letting it get in the way and thus prevent the words being found. There is a special quality of reflective silence within a relationship, however, which can enable the griever to find his own words. This silence is not an empty silence but contains acceptance and understanding. This lets the bereaved know that you value them and what they have to say about their experience of loss. It also tells them, without words, that you know they must struggle to find their own words for their sorrow. As you listen and give attention they will begin to trust you not to rush in with the useless platitude or controlling question and will be able to risk sharing more of their feelings with you.

When you consider this aspect of 'being-with' another in their search to express their sorrow, you need to pay attention to a number of ways in which you or the client can be distracted. These are listed in Table 9.2.

Table 9.2 Distractions to good listening

External distractions	– things in the world, in the room
Distractions in your own behaviour	– posture, eye contact, facial expression
Distractions from your attitudes	– some of your own personal attitudes may get in the way of listening
Distractions in your feelings	– your own unresolved losses; your own fears and anxiety; unexpressed messages about the relationship between client and counsellor

External distractions

You may need to use your confidence as a counsellor to make sure that the environment of counselling is conducive to the work, even if it has to be in other people's homes.

Telephones, televisions, radios, cooking, callers, active animals or small children can be distracting and it is necessary to arrange for these things not to intrude, whatever the situation. If the client is reluctant to remove distractions you may be picking up their fear of their own feelings. You need to pay attention to this fear.

Distractions in your own behaviour

An open and relaxed posture (not crossed arms or legs) is often perceived as more accepting and trustworthy. Eye contact is important, not intermittent or staring, but gently sensing how much eye contact can be tolerated. Facial expression is also important; raised eyebrows or grimaces can be understood as expressions of disapproval even though not intended in this way. A smile may be reassuring as a welcome, but would be inappropriate as a response to feelings of sadness. It is worth remembering that fear, helplessness or sometimes anger may lurk behind a smile which is 'stuck'; both in yourself and in your client.

Attitudinal distractions

In Table 2.1 we summed up the basic attitudes of counselling as the attitudes of real acceptance, empathic understanding and genuineness. People are more likely to reveal themselves to counsellors who demonstrate these attitudes and are perceived as trustworthy. As humans, we seem to be more comfortable with and ready to trust people who we think are like ourselves. People are less likely to trust those in whom they detect prejudices.

It is important for counsellors to find out as much as they can about their own prejudices and reactions to those who are different from themselves. Exercise 9.1 offers you a chance to find out more about your own reactions and attitudes to people whom you perceive as either similar or different to yourself.

Exercise 9.1 Listening to your own reactions and distractions

Imagine you are entering a counselling relationship with each of these nine people and try to conjure up a picture of each person in your mind's eye. Think through your feelings and reactions to each one. *Do not analyse the situation* but focus on your own feelings and reactions. Then try to rate each situation according to the difficulty you might have in really listening to that person. Rate them according to the following scale:

0 = No problem in listening
1 = Slight problem in listening
2 = Considerable problem in listening

Sketches   *Rating*

1 Jean (55) is a grandmother who was recently knocked down by a drunken driver. Her daughter Mary and family live 40 miles away and her son Frank is out of touch after a difficult divorce. Jean was quite badly injured but insists she cannot stay in hospital and seems fearful of all hospital routine.

2 George (55) is a successful businessman whose wife died six months ago. He implies that he was a bit of a 'womaniser' and goes on to tell you that he had a mistress until 6 weeks after his wife's death. He broke off the relationship out of guilt about his mistress's contribution to his wife's death. He is now lonely and remorseful.

3 Josie (27) is a beautiful young woman whose common-law husband, Dean, the father of two of her four children, recently disappeared without trace. She constantly complains about him and about living in a situation where she feels her rights are frequently undermined. She is angry and resentful.

4 Joe's mother, Katherine, died 18 months ago from cancer. He was an only child and his father, Joseph, left when Joe was 2. Joe is now 22, single, unemployed and says he can't see any reason to work; the state owes him money after all his troubles. He seems listless and lifeless.

5 Oliver (24) has just been told that he has leukaemia. He has just graduated in philosophy and was hoping to train as a social worker. He is engaged to Angie (also 24) who has just graduated in French. He seems numb.

Exercise 9.1 (continued)

6 Fatima (19) has just been told of her father's decision that she should marry Ismail. She tells you that she loves Rahindra but that she cannot marry him for he belongs to the wrong religious group. Her father's will must be respected, she says, without rancour. Her sadness seems to fill the room.

7 Alice (44) is the mother of Brendan (22) who died six weeks ago from Aids, contracted as a result of using infected needles to inject heroin. Her husband Fred had expelled him from their home three years ago when he had learned of the addiction. Fred cannot cope with Alice's grief. Alice seems on the verge of hysteria.

8 Clive (52) is an upright, uptight bachelor who recently retired from the armed forces. His dog, Matilda, who was his only companion, had become lame and was run over and killed by a bus when running out of Jubilee Park next to his house. He keeps talking angrily about how awful the weather is.

9 Lizzie (36) has been married to Frank since just before the birth of their first child. They were both 18 when they married. Frank is a workaholic and Lizzie looks after him and their two children. She's been depressed off and on for most of their marriage but now is feeling so low that suicide seems the only option.

Having rated each person for ease of listening:
1 write down your immediate attitudes to each person in this exercise; and
2 for those rated 1 and 2, think of the reasons why you would be distracted from listening accurately to that person. What assumptions might you be making about the kinds of people you think you know least?

Are there any other characteristics you can think of which might distract you from active listening?

Exercise 9.1 (continued)

What assumptions have you made about the ethnic origins of the people described here? In what ways might a person's ethnic origin and/or colour of skin influence your listening?

You should also try to 'get inside the skin' of the people described here and see how closely you can identify with them. See if you can get inside them enough to experience what they are feeling. These feelings might be different from the feelings you identified in your own reactions to the individuals.

Wherever possible, discuss your answers with a colleague or fellow counsellor.

Having done this exercise it is worth thinking about what you discovered about yourself and what steps you might take to enlarge your experience of human beings who are different from you. You may then be able to identify things which distract you from maintaining the counselling attitudes. If you discover attitudinal distractions in yourself it is worth thinking about your particular prejudices. Discussing these with a non-judgemental friend may help you understand which attitudes can be changed. If some seem unchangeable you may want to think how to refer such a client to someone less prejudiced in that area.

Distractions in your feelings

This distraction is somewhat different from the other three. Distracting noises, behaviour and attitudes interfere with our capacity to listen and it is important to find ways to lessen them. Distraction caused by our feelings usually has two components. One of these can, like the other distractions, interfere with the counselling relationship, while the other component can be a useful source of understanding.

The first component of a feeling distraction relates to feelings in us about our past life and losses, and it is in this area that *loss* counselling can be especially challenging. When you really listen to a grieving person it may stir up painful feelings from your past losses. These feelings may also evoke fear about things which could or might happen in the future to you or those you love. Listening to bereaved people, for instance, may heighten your awareness of your own mortality. It is for these reasons that it is important that you come to terms with your own fears and feelings about the losses in your own life and about your attitudes to death, so that these feelings do not interfere with your listening. Understanding your own losses will also help you to determine your limitations in terms of whom you can help at any particular time.

The other component of the feeling distraction may be a feeling not recognised though actually experienced by the client. This can be a useful message in understanding the counselling relationship and is discussed further in chapters 13 and 15. Actually letting yourself experience the various feelings and being aware that there are two different components is a very important part of counselling training and counselling supervision.

REFLECTING EXPERIENCE AND FEELINGS

When we are able to listen openly to another person and to enter their world without judgement and with acute sensitivity to their experiences and feelings, then we could be said to be offering empathic listening (see Table 2.1). Another way of expressing empathy can be found in reflecting. Reflecting happens at many levels. At its most basic it means restating in your words the literal meaning, as you understand it, of what your client has just said. At the beginning this idea of reflection may seem highly artificial. It may also seem very difficult when faced with choices about how to understand all the messages coming from your client, as well as choices about how to formulate your response. As with the bicycle, in the early stages you are acutely aware of these choices, but as you practise, the conscious choices recede from awareness and are made on a less conscious level. This seems to allow balanced and more natural or spontaneous responses to develop.

A good reflection does not mean just the mechanical repetition of the words you have heard. It means finding your own words to reflect back to the person the sense of what they have said, both at the level of the content and of the feelings expressed. If you also use an intonation which is tentative this allows the client to disagree or put you right or, indeed, put themselves right as they begin to understand themselves more clearly. In Exercise 9.2 we give you an opportunity to practise accurate reflection.

Exercise 9.2 Accurate reflection

Restate in different words, and in clear and simple language, the literal meaning of the client's statements.

Try them out loud, paying attention to voice quality (gentleness, tentative style, etc.) as well as to intonation (the rise and fall of the voice).

EXAMPLE

Susan: My husband was a fine man. His sudden death was a great shock. I still miss him terribly.

One of many possible responses from the counsellor might be:

Counsellor: Your husband's unexpected death really shook you to the core. You still miss him terribly.

Reflect in your own words the sense of client's message.

1 Joe: I thought I was prepared for my mother's death but ever since she passed away I've been thinking that life is not worth living.

Counsellor:

2 Robin: Ever since my parents' divorce I've been feeling angry and resentful but at last I'm beginning to see that not having them together is not necessarily the end of my life, I suppose.

Counsellor:

Exercise 9.2 (continued)

3 Lizzie: I'm feeling so depressed. Just getting through the day is an enormous effort. I don't think I'll ever get on top of things now that Frank's gone.

Counsellor:

4 Josie: Since Dean disappeared my mother says 'do this', my father says 'do that', and my sister says 'do something else'. Now I'm feeling totally confused.

Counsellor:

In these examples in Exercise 9.2 the clients have all been able to express fairly clearly what they were feeling using the feeling words themselves. People are not always so articulate, lucid or helpful and it is sometimes up to the counsellor to find the 'feeling-word' which expresses the sense of what is being communicated. Having one's feelings understood, accepted and tentatively put into words can be a very affirming experience. This non-judgemental attitude to feelings can be expressed:

a) by voicing the feeling-word in a warm tone and with rising intonation.
b) by linking the feeling-word with the situation which appears to have given rise to the feelings. This gives a 'sense' and rightness to the feelings in their context.

In order to feel at home in the language of feelings, you need a large range of feeling-words at your disposal. For a preliminary list of such words see Table 9.3. You can add to this list from your own experiences of counselling, of television, of the theatre, of books, of films and of life itself.

Table 9.3 Feeling-words

Angry	Fearful	Excited	Frantic	Lonely
Sad	Frustrated	Loving	Helpless	Happy
Furious	Warm	Desperate	Accused	Listless
Anxious	Tense	Hating	Numb	Injured
Frightened	Terrified	Cold	Tentative	Battered
Resentful	Annoyed	Icy	Hurt	Pierced
Hopeless	Cross	Despairing	Guilty	Valued

Exercise 9.3 gives you the opportunity to find the feeling-words hidden in the statements.

Exercise 9.3 Reflecting feelings

a) **See if you can guess at the feeling-word which the statement might be trying to express. Reflect it back out loud with a warm tone and rising intonation just to experience this for yourself. It may help to make a tape-recording of yourself.**
b) **See if you can link the feeling to what you have heard in a way that 'makes sense' for the client.**

Example

William: I said some awful things to Thomas the day before his accident. I can't get them out of my mind.

Counsellor: a) ... guilt?   or   ... remorse?
            b) It sounds as though you've been feeling guilty about the things you said to Thomas and you can't get them out of your mind.

1 Alice: What could I have done to deserve having my son die?

Counsellor:

2 Joe: I can't go on like this... I've been thinking of chucking it all in.

Counsellor:

3 George: The doctor who operated on my wife was an incompetent fool.

Counsellor:

Exercise 9.3 (continued)

4 Oliver: Everything is in a muddle. I can't seem to make any decisions.

Counsellor:

5 Christopher:
Just how do you think you can help me? Do you know what it feels like to have your lover die? Can you give him back to me?

Counsellor:

6 Jean: What could have pushed Lizzie that far? Was it a cry for help or did she really *mean* to die? Why did she do it? What can I say to her?

Counsellor:

7 Fatima: I love Rahindra deeply but he is not one of us. A girl must obey her father. I expect I will manage.

Counsellor:

Listening and sensing the feelings behind the words is sometimes called 'listening for the music behind the words'. Of course, giving you dry words on a printed page gives you very little sense of the music behind them because we pick up the song not only through words but through intonation, voice quality, gestures, facial expression, posture, dress and other features.

We cannot create the 'music' in this book but we can try to listen for the music behind the words with real people. Take time to pick up the signals and sense the feeling state of those around you from time to time. You can always check it out with them!

REFLECTING USING DIFFERENT LEVELS OF EMPATHY

As well as the music behind the words there is often a different tune we begin to hear or sense. Sometimes this tune may seem to be at odds, or out of harmony, with the main music. There may be, for instance, angry feelings lurking under the sadness, or a discrepancy between gesture and word or even a discrepancy between the meaning of the words and the way in which they are expressed. When we notice this we are sensing a different tune behind the main music.

This sensing of the different tune of which the speaker may be only very dimly aware is sometimes called 'empathy at the edge of awareness' (Mearns and Thorne, 1988). In grief the feelings at the edge of awareness may be those which are the most frightening or most painful to experience. Sensing these feelings and allowing their expression is very helpful to the grief process. It is wise, however, to approach them with gentleness and care as they are the feelings which have 'needed' to be hidden and of which the griever may be afraid.

We shall call this kind of reflecting, 'reflecting with deeper empathy'. In our next example we give possible responses, at four so-called different levels of empathy. Again these responses can seem artificial out of context and they can only begin to indicate what is meant by deeper levels of empathy in the whole context of a counselling relationship practice. There is a real danger that these minimal context examples give an impression of ease and simplicity to a set of responses, which in practice are much more complex. They can, for example, give no indication of the importance of pacing in the flow between counsellor and griever. Nor can they demonstrate the inestimable value of receptive silence which forms such an intrinsic part of the empathic response. For all their shortcomings, however, these examples offer a way of starting to look at the complex response we have called deeper empathy.

Example of empathy levels

Susan: He left so suddenly leaving me with the children, the bills and the house half painted. Why did he leave me all on my own?... Well, I suppose I'll manage... (grits teeth)... I will cope then. I'll have to. I'm strong enough.

Counsellor's response:

Empathy 0: It's God's will and there's no explaining it!

Empathy 1: What a shock for you!

Empathy 2: You must be feeling really abandoned through his sudden absence and I expect you're angry because you're having to deal with so much on your own.

Empathy 3: You must be feeling really abandoned through his sudden absence and I expect you're angry because you're having to deal with so much on your own ... but, I see you're gritting your teeth as though perhaps you were frightened of something?

In this example the empathy level 0 response shows no empathy at all and we could understand this response as meaning something like, 'I think I hear pain and I don't want to feel pain so let's change the subject', or 'I think I hear anger or even envy and I don't want to know about them either.' Whatever it does mean for the counsellor, there is no sense of understanding the client's perceptual world.

The empathy level 1 response indicates some understanding of the sense of shock which is being experienced but it could be expressing the counsellor's shock with the 'for you' just tagged on at the end. The tone of voice would make a big difference to the way these words were understood.

The empathy level 2 response shows a recognition of the feelings of abandonment and of anger, and links them with the experience. It is a good empathic response and the most basic counsellor response.

The level 3 response adds to the level 2 response the sense, presumably picked up from the client, that she might also be frightened by what had happened and this extra level of understanding may enable her to recognise and face her fears about, for instance, surviving on her own.

In Exercise 9.4 you can assess the different levels of empathy shown by the counsellor.

Exercise 9.4 Levels of empathy exercise

Rank the jumbled empathic responses into their most appropriate levels.

Joe: I thought I was prepared for my mother's death but ever since she passed away I've been feeling down and thinking that (getting louder) life's not worth living.

Responses   *Rank*

a) You'd thought you were ready for her death but since then you've been feeling really low and wondering if you want to go on living... But I wonder ... whether you're perhaps a bit angry that things haven't gone the way you expected, the way you were prepared for...?

b) It was a shock all the same.

c) You thought you were ready for her death but since it actually happened you've been feeling low and not sure if life is worth living.

d) Death comes to us all, doesn't it?

(Key: a = 3, b = 1, c = 2, d = 0)

Robin: Ever since my parent's divorce I've been angry and resentful. Why should I have to suffer just because they can't manage to get along with one another and quarrel all the time? But I suppose I'm beginning to see that their being apart is not necessarily the end... (rising intonation).

Responses   *Rank*

a) You have to get on with your life.

b) Since they divorced you've felt angry and resentful about their inability to get on with one another. Now you're thinking that their being apart may not be the end for you.

c) It must be very difficult for you now.

d) Since they divorced you've felt angry and resentful about their inability to get on with one another. Now you're thinking that their being apart may not be the end... and perhaps... there's a ray of hope that things may eventually start to feel easier now that they're apart and not quarrelling all the time?

(Key: a = 0, b = 2, c = 1, d = 3)

Exercise 9.4 (continued)

Josie: Since Dean left me my mother says 'do this', my father says 'do that' and my sister says 'do something else'! Now I'm feeling totally confused.

Responses   *Rank*

a) Since he jilted you, everyone's been saying something different and now you're feeling totally confused.

b) He wasn't much use anyway.

c) That's upsetting for you.

d) Since he finished with you, your mother's been saying 'do this', your father says 'do that' and your sister says 'do something else' again. Now you're feeling totally confused ... and, well, you look so sad. I wonder if there are some really sad, painful feelings behind all the confusion?

(Key: a = 2, b = 0, c = 1, d = 3)

Angie: I feel so angry that Oliver should have got leukaemia. What a waste of a life! And he is going to die – why do they have to keep giving him more and more treatment at the hospital? I wouldn't stand for it – why couldn't it be me who got leukaemia?

Response   *Rank*

a) You're feeling really angry that Oliver should have become so ill.

b) Life's not fair, is it?

c) It sounds as though you're angry that Oliver is ill and angry with the doctors who seem not to accept that Oliver is dying. You wish that he could be left in peace.

d) You are angry that Oliver is ill and can't understand why it's him... I wonder if you think it should have been you and ... perhaps you feel guilty ... even helpless that it isn't you who has got leukaemia.

(Key: a = 1, b = 0, c = 2, d = 3)

Empathic listening is the bread-and-butter work of loss counselling and is likely to facilitate the main grief work of a session. In the next chapter the management of beginnings and endings, together with what they might mean, gives a frame or boundary for the work.

SUMMARY

1   The counselling attitudes can enable grievers to be less frightened and less condemning of the feelings they experience as part of grief.
2   Counselling skills, learned separately, are later integrated more naturally into practice in a way that is responsive to the grieving person.
3   Reflective listening can enable grievers to find their own words to express their loss. It is easy to be distracted from this reflective listening, particularly in the area of feelings arising in the listener.
4   Reflecting the client's experience and feeling in words can be very affirming. It can help clients to accept the validity of their own feelings.
5   More deeply empathic responses pick up feelings at the edge of awareness. The griever may have 'needed' to keep certain feelings out of full awareness; their recognition and reflection will require care and consideration.

10

FURTHER LOSS COUNSELLING SKILLS

In previous chapters we saw how non-judgemental attitudes of acceptance and empathic responding can offer an environment of relative safety where the often frightening feelings associated with loss can be understood, validated and contained. 'Contained' here means two things. First and foremost that the feelings find a place or container in which they can be safely held. A second meaning of containment here is that misconceptions, through lack of knowledge or information about the mourning process, are clarified and explained. Without clarification these misconceptions can cause a lot of fear. First we shall consider the 'container' as a safe place.

SETTING LIMITS OR BOUNDARIES

Containers, like counselling sessions, need limits or boundaries. The enclosed space of the counselling session, safe from intruders either in person or on the telephone, constitutes one aspect of the 'container'. The stretch of time between the beginning and end of the session is a further aspect of the container. Time, and meanings associated with time, are often particularly significant for those who have suffered a loss. Time-past was the time which contained that which was valued and then lost, time-now (in the session) is the time in which the feelings about that loss are allowed to emerge and time-future has to be faced without that which was lost.

When a person has suffered a loss they also suffer a distortion in their perception of time and space. This distortion varies in intensity between being merely unnerving for some people, to chaotic and frightening for others. Setting clear time limits or boundaries can contribute greatly to a feeling of safety and predictability, even though it can feel a little odd or even 'heartless' to the starter counsellor. Of course boundaries need to be negotiable in certain circumstances and flexible in others, but they need to be clear and to be openly talked about. This is not in order to exercise power over the other person, but in order to create a framework within which power can be shared and safety enhanced. The safety and predictability create clear time and space within which strong feelings can be shared and contained.

Beginnings: sessions and relationships

Sometimes the first 'loss' session takes place within the context of a more-or-less established professional relationship, though perhaps of a different kind, and the loss material is signalled in a particular way. When loss material is signalled it is usually worth re-establishing or recontracting the time boundary to enhance the safety of the 'container'. This is illustrated in the next example.

> Sonia is a worker in a children's home. Mrs Murphy, who visits her son Seamus in the home on a regular basis, has always been punctual, competent and cheerful, if anything perhaps too cheerful. Sonia noticed that recently Mrs Murphy has been forgetting her son's special food. When Mrs Murphy started to tell Sonia about the accident which led to Seamus's handicap, Sonia could sense Mrs Murphy's need to tell her of her grief. She suggested warmly and firmly that they should go to a nearby office for half an hour. Having arranged for someone else to cover for her, Sonia knew that she would not be interrupted and would be able to give Mrs Murphy her undivided attention for the half hour she knew she had created. This 'safe-container' helped Mrs Murphy get on with what she needed to share.

The beginning of the first session is, however, more often the beginning of the counselling relationship and the openings of further sessions take place within the context of this relationship which has already begun.

Harry has arranged to see you at 11 a.m. for the first time. Each new client brings an entirely new world into your work. You may or may not have information about Harry, but in one sense you know nothing about his world nor about his expectations of you. So you do not even know what questions it might be appropriate to ask. Even 'How can I help you?' implies that 'help' (whatever that means to Harry or to you) is what he's expecting and implies also that 'I' might be able to supply that from a position of power or 'superior' knowledge. Counselling may indeed be a very helpful way-of-being with someone in distress and grappling with strong feelings, but offering 'help' only exacerbates the already unequal power relationship in counselling, and might imply that you were going to do the work.

We do not know anything about Harry, but what we do know is that you are prepared to be there with him, uninterruptedly, for a certain time period. Let us say, for instance, that you are able to give him half an hour. We are also assuming, for the moment, that he wants to be with you for that amount of time. You will, of course, find your own personal way of opening your first sessions, but here are some possible opening phrases.

Possible openings

1 Hello Harry. We have 30 minutes together...
2 Hello Harry. We have 30 minutes together... I wonder what has brought you here?
3 Hello Harry. We have 30 minutes together... Where would you like to start?
4 Hello Harry. You are free to start when you are ready ... we have about 30 minutes together.

In example 1 simply setting the time boundary in a warm and confident manner, with its implication of a predictable space and time, may be enough in itself to allow Harry to get started where he wishes. If he wants, or needs more encouragement, then any of the other examples would probably help him get started and also recognise and put into words the fact that the time is for him. It also indicates that you are not in the business of trying to control him; your limit, as opposed to control, is the time boundary. Getting straight down to business and avoiding social chat about the weather or his journey indicates to Harry your recognition of the seriousness of what he is bringing. This first session opening can set a pattern for future session openings. As Harry gets used to the amount of time he has with you, whether 10 or 50 minutes, it may be enough simply to say: 'Hello Harry, where would you like to start today?' and, as trust grows you may find that 'Hello Harry...?' is all that is necessary. It may be especially useful for him to have a consistent amount of time with you on each occasion if this is manageable.

Of course not all sessions start so easily; for some people the feelings are so strong they are expressed almost before the session has started. Let us consider the start of counselling with Angie (Exercise 9.4) who is engaged to be married to Oliver (Exercises 9.1 and 9.3). Oliver is dying of an incurable form of leukaemia. He is still in hospital but is being allowed home to die. This session opens very abruptly with Angie's feelings so near the surface and ready for expression, that she breaks in before the counsellor has finished speaking.

Example of a tricky opening

Counsellor: Hello Angie, we have 30 minutes toge...
Angie: So what use is that going to be? All the time in the world won't bring Oliver back!
You can't bring him back, can you?
Counsellor: (Gently and slowly) No, you're absolutely right, I can't bring him back. What I *can* offer you is some time to look at your very frightening situation.

The counsellor's response arises out of the attitude of genuineness, which recognises the counsellor's helplessness in facing the reality of Oliver's imminent death. The slow and gentle tone also recognises the sadness and untimely nature of Oliver's death. This tone will also have a calming effect on Angie who is caught up in anger and panic. The clarity of the time boundaries means Angie can have at least some control over how she uses the session. It also means that if she chooses to talk about and feel her fear and anger about the approaching death, it will be contained by the time limit. By choosing the word 'frightening' the counsellor brings an appropriate feeling-word to the situation. This gives Angie a sense of recognition and perhaps enables her to face her frightening feelings. Under the anger may well be helplessness and despair. This 'sense of recognition' may help Angie to begin to trust her counsellor, even at a time when trust of anyone must be difficult for her.

In the next examples different counsellors use their empathy and 'gut-feelings' to sense what the clients are feeling and then put this into words.

Other examples of openings

Dan

Counsellor:	Hello Dan, we have 30 minutes together.
Dan:	(Seems to shrink down inside his coat which he has kept on. He says nothing)
Counsellor:	(After a few moments, sensing his apprehension and struggle for words) I suppose it's not easy to begin ... some things are really difficult to put into words.

Sharon

Counsellor:	Hello Sharon, we have 30 minutes together.
Sharon:	Yes, I know! (falling intonation)
Counsellor:	(Sensing her discomfort and possible rebellion) I expect it feels pretty uncomfortable having to come along and see me like this, and ... well, I don't know, but perhaps feeling you're expected to do what I want?

Andy

Counsellor:	Hello Andy, we have 30 minutes together.
Andy:	Yes (softly and obligingly with rising intonation).
Counsellor:	(After a few moments, sensing his shyness and apparent expectations of something) I guess it feels pretty odd coming to talk to a strange person like me and not knowing what to expect – mm?

In all these examples of beginning a session the counsellor tries to convey to the client the wish to explore together and try to understand more of the client's world without imposing her own will or agenda. The counsellor also recognises that she is a part of this exploratory process.

Endings: sessions and relationships

In writing about beginnings we could treat the beginning of the session and the relationship as one broad topic. We cannot do this so readily with endings for a number of reasons. Usually the end of the first counselling session is not the end of the relationship. Therefore session endings will be different from relationship endings, although there will also be similarities. In addition most of us have much stronger and more complex feelings associated with endings than with beginnings. You only have to watch farewells at railway stations or airports to see examples of this. Less obvious perhaps is that the ending of the counselling relationship, and the consequent loss of intimacy, may reflect the very loss which the person has come to grieve. This 'reflected loss' may also be present towards the end of each counselling session and sometimes makes bereavement counselling sessions particularly difficult to end. This reflected loss is, of course, not the same as the 'original loss' and the counsellor may need to remember that the end of the session does not 'make the loss worse'. On the contrary, it may be the one ending over which the client can have more-or-less manageable feelings. What is important is to recognise, validate and contain such feelings re-evoked through the ending of the session.

Session endings

Let us return to our sessions with Angie. After the rather tricky beginning, Angie realised that her anger was acceptable to the counsellor after all. As her panic subsided she was able to face and experience strong, angry feelings about Oliver's death and the way his death seemed to make a mockery of her health and liveliness. She also gained more understanding about Oliver's mother's anger and her apparent resentfulness of Angie's blooming health. Gradually she was able to become involved with the plans to allow Oliver to die at home.

The end of the first session had been relatively straightforward. The counsellor had reminded Angie of the time about 10 minutes before the end of the session. Angie had expressed surprise that the time had passed so quickly and became aware of how relieved she was to have shared her angry feelings. She also felt she had laid down a burden of guilt about her anger. She seemed quite pleased to finish that session.

However, during the sixth session when considerably more trust had developed with her counsellor, Angie started to talk about her rather perturbing feelings. She was beginning to wish that it could all be over for Oliver, yet at the same time desperately wishing that Oliver would not die and leave her. Angie was still struggling with this conflict of feelings when the counsellor pointed out, as was usual, that it was 10 minutes to the end of the session. Angie did not seem to notice this and went on without stopping. The counsellor again reminded Angie of the time after a further 5 minutes, while recognising verbally that Angie was struggling with something very important. Angie ignored him. The counsellor, wondering briefly how he would ever end this session, reflected on this feeling of slight panic in himself. He began to realise that Angie's mixed and ambivalent feelings about the end of her relationship with Oliver were probably being experienced in the ending of this session. He wondered to himself whether it were possible that in Angie's world out there with Oliver, she had no control over the ending of the relationship; but in here she was going to exert all the control she could muster and see how long she could put off the dreaded ending. It was difficult to stop Angie's flow and the counsellor was not sure that he had understood what Angie was experiencing but he sensed it must be about 'endings'. An example of how he used this idea is shown next.

Example of a difficult session ending

Counsellor: Angie, (louder) Angie! Perhaps it feels uncomfortable when I interrupt you like this but I have something important I want to say to you... Both of us are having difficulty in finishing this session at the time we have agreed. I am wondering whether some of the difficulties of ending the relationship with Oliver are making it particularly difficult to end our session today? We don't have time to pursue this now but it might be very useful for us to look at this difficulty early on in next session. As we finish today (eye contact) I recognise that I am leaving you with a lot of very unresolved and difficult feelings... I will see you on *Friday* at the usual time.

It takes energy and planning to make a response that cuts in on a client who is preoccupied. The suggested response in the example focuses on a number of issues.

First it recognises Angie's discomfort in being interrupted. The counsellor accepts that he and Angie share the difficulty with the ending. This values Angie and takes the 'difficulty' off any one individual's shoulders and makes it clear that this 'difficulty' has a meaning. This allows both the counsellor and Angie to consider the difficulty without either of them being burdened by it. Then the counsellor confirms the agreement about the time of the ending. This reminds Angie of the agreed and predictable nature of the sessions, thus offering her something secure, which is particularly important when she cannot predict how or when Oliver will die. Finally the counsellor highlights a possible parallel between the difficulty in ending the session and the difficult and painful ending of the relationship with Oliver.

Note that the counsellor does not extend the session any further. It is perhaps tempting to offer more time when we sense someone is very needy. However, this has to be weighed up against the burden of disorganisation and stress for the counsellor and even more importantly the burden of unnecessary guilt for the griever, who may feel she 'stole' time from the counsellor. Another reason for stopping the session is that the counsellor suspects that Angie may want to take control of the session just as she wants to control Oliver's dying. Letting Angie wrest the control of the ending might lead her to imagine that she can actually control Oliver's dying. This fantasy would not be useful to her. However, it might well be useful to explore this fantasy in words in the following session. From this exploration Angie will discover that endings cannot necessarily be controlled, but the feelings about the endings can be worked on before the ending of the relationship takes place.

During the following sessions Angie did recognise her mixed feelings. She began to face the meaning of Oliver's death and the fact that she would have many months of grief ahead of her. She then became able to think about how she might say 'goodbye' to Oliver. This included thinking about and planning what she still wanted to do and say to Oliver while he was still alive.

Ending the relationship

Clients usually raise the question of ending the relationship when they feel ready for it. Raising the question of ending their relationship with a counsellor may, as already mentioned, remind them of loss in general and, in particular, may reflect the very loss they are trying to grieve. This recognition often seems to set them back as they go through a separate process of grief for the loss of the counsellor. However, this very grieving for the counsellor is usually enormously healing, and in working through this loss together the 'old wound' will also be grieved.

This was indeed what happened with Angie. After Oliver had died and many months of grief had passed, Angie began to think of doing things for herself again and beginning to meet new people. But just as life seemed to be going so much better for Angie, and the counsellor was wondering about mentioning the ending of the counselling relationship, so the sessions again began to get more difficult to end. This time Angie herself noticed the difficulty and then remembered a dream she had had of seeing the counsellor off on a large ship and waving white handkerchiefs. On waking she had felt terribly sad. She herself made the connection between the dream and the session. Inside herself she felt ready to end the relationship with the counsellor, but the sadness of ending reminded her of her grief and longing for Oliver and left her feeling almost overwhelmed.

The counsellor recognised Angie's sadness but also pointed out that they shared the sadness at the ending of the relationship. In the subsequent sessions he shared with Angie how much he had valued being allowed to be alongside her in her grief and struggle. Finally the counsellor reflected on how the sadness would always be a part of Angie and would be something she would share with other people in her life. Indeed, in grieving for Oliver she had found new depth and sensitivity. They parted company aware of both sadness and excitement as Angie faced the world again. We shall pick up Angie's story again in chapter 15.

CLARIFICATIONS

You will be aware from Angie's, and also perhaps from your own experiences, that certain reactions to loss can be frightening. Usually this fear can be lessened through the counsellor's acceptance of the expression of the fear. Sometimes lack of knowledge or lack of information exacerbates fear, in which case some form of clarification of the client's misunderstanding or a piece of relevant information may be very useful. This is a delicate task, as it can threaten the exercise of shared control and power and can make the client feel powerless. None the less there are certain kinds of information related to bereavement and other kinds of loss which can reduce fear and isolation, thereby actually empowering the client to proceed with the grieving.

Clarifying hallucinations

We mentioned in chapter 3 that the disbelief that someone is lost often manifests itself in hallucination. In the case of Anne she thought she saw James in the street almost a year after he had died. Angie's counsellor provides us with an example of how a counsellor might give information to a client in order to clarify and understand a similar experience.

Giving information about an hallucination

One day not long after Oliver's death Angie arrived trembling with fright and told the counsellor what had happened.

Angie: I was on the bus going along Victoria Road and just waiting to get off by Central Library. I was not thinking of anything in particular when suddenly I saw

Oliver walking along the pavement. I shouted and leapt off the bus. Fortunately it was slowing down or I'd have killed myself – as it was, I nearly got run over and hurt my ankle quite badly. I knew I'd seen him but as I sat there on the pavement of course I began to realise that he was dead. An old lady came and asked me if I was all right. I must have been crying and I told her I'd seen Oliver. She didn't seem particularly surprised about Oliver but more surprised that I'd leapt off the bus. I must be going mad. I'm so sure I saw him. Perhaps I'm crazy. It was such a shock seeing him like that. Am I going mad?

Counsellor:	Angie... (gently and slowly) people who've lost someone close to them sometimes do 'see' them suddenly like that...	Clarifying through information giving
	It can be very frightening and disorientating.	Link with feeling
Angie:	You mean I'm not the only one?	
Counsellor:	(Shakes head)	
Angie:	Then perhaps I'm not going mad – yes, it was very frightening and I feel quite shaken up by it...	

The task of the counsellor is to find a way to make it clear that the event is perfectly 'normal', while not denying the particular experience of the individual. In this example this is done by using the word 'people'. The counsellor then recognises the metaphoric use of the word 'see'. Having given the information it is important to link back into the person's feelings. It might also be important to recognise the ankle pain!

Clarifying behaviour

This 'carrying-around-in-our-head' of something familiar is, of course, not restricted to the bereaved and can occur whilst awake or in dreams. We are all familiar with waking up at the normal workday time when on holiday and wondering where we are, or with carrying on a routine when it is no longer necessary. It is as though we are still carrying around the comfort of the familiar routine until we can tackle the change. The next example illustrates this and demonstrates one way of helping someone recognise what is happening.

Giving information about behaviour

Sheila was visiting her GP with lower back pain shortly after her youngest child, Ruth, left for university. Her GP could find no obvious organic cause for the back pain and, noticing Sheila's apprehension about leaving the surgery, asked her what else was worrying her.

Sheila: Well you see, I keep dreaming that Ruth's still here and then I wake up as usual at 7.30 a.m. and I go straight into her room and shout 'Ruth, time to get up!' It's quite dotty, but I do feel as if she's here when I wake up and just can't seem to remember that she's gone to university.

Doctor: Of course you feel as if she's still at home, that's quite natural. Many people feel as if the person who has gone away is still there. (Seeing relief on Sheila's face.) I expect you miss her enormously.

Sheila: Yes, I keep worrying about whether she'll be all right, whether she'll make friends, whether she'll manage on her grant, whether she's happy...

Doctor: I understand your worries. Ruth has a lot of new challenges and new experiences to savour... But you have the challenge of learning to live without Ruth, of how to live without waking her every morning. You must be feeling very sad and empty without her.

Sheila was thus able to feel surer that she was not going mad and to recognise that she too had a big challenge ahead; that of managing and enjoying term-time life without Ruth. Her feelings of sadness and emptiness were also recognised. This helped Sheila to recognise and grieve her loss and enabled her to feel more resourceful in herself.

Clarifying dreams

The desire for a return to a former time so as not to have to bear what is happening in the present can also manifest itself in dreams. In the following example it is important to recognise the feelings evoked by the dream and those evoked by the information being given.

Giving information about a dream

You will remember Robin Clark (Table 8.1 and Exercises 9.2 and 9.4) whose mother Lizzie was severely depressed in 1991 and whose parents Frank and Lizzie were divorcing two years later. The divorce was hard for him to accept.

Robin: It seems so silly. I had this dream ... it was so realistic. My parents had got together again and were reconciling their differences. My father had come back ... we

107

were a family again sitting round the table... Then when I woke up I really believed it. I just could not believe it wasn't true. I felt so guilty for not wanting to let them separate, or let him go off to a better life. I must be crazy...?

Counsellor: Robin, many people whose parents are divorcing feel like that and naturally enough, dream of the reconciliation they had longed for. Of course you don't want them to separate but you have very little power to alter that situation... } Information to clarify a) Robin not crazy b) Robin powerless

Robin: (Reflectively) I suppose so.

Counsellor: Indeed you might perhaps find yourself feeling angry as well as helpless about your situation? } Recognition of angry or helpless feelings at the edge of awareness, possibly covered by the more 'acceptable' guilty feeling

In this example it is likely that when Robin heard from the counsellor that he was in reality powerless to change the situation, he would have felt recognised, understood and validated. He could then begin to see that his wishes were quite natural and that he was not guilty for his feelings and longings. This might allow him to feel the natural anger that an adolescent would feel towards divorcing parents, which in turn would enable him to start to accept the real separation. After that the dreams of reconciliation would begin to fade.

Clarifying beliefs

It is quite common for anyone coping with an unacceptable situation to construct incorrect beliefs to help them cope with the loss as the following example illustrates.

Giving information about an incorrect belief

Frank (Table 8.1) had left the family quite overpowered by feelings of guilt and helplessness. To try to manage these feelings he had constructed a belief that Lizzie was 'the better parent', that Lizzie 'was the person they needed, not him' and that if he left them alone this would 'help Lizzie feel good about herself'. It also transpired that Frank was frightened of Lizzie's underlying anger and was also frightened of a more overt anger in his daughter Jenny. Robin *seemed* to be accepting things more easily.

Frank:	It's hopeless, there's no point in trying to relate to the children. They are better off with their mother. She needs them more than I do ... and anyway I'm a pretty useless father...	
Counsellor:	Frank, fathers often feel this way in your situation and I can understand you're trying to believe that you're not an important part of their lives.	General information
	Perhaps that belief, though indeed painful, is less painful	Recognising feelings
	than accepting the loss of the family as you knew it and working out new ways of being with your children.	Challenging beliefs
Frank:	Er, well, yes. I suppose it's true...	
Counsellor:	I guess that's a very painful recognition.	Recognising feelings again

When Frank was able to recognise and work through his own pain and helplessness and then his anger about the separations, he grew less frightened of Lizzie's underlying anger and less guilty. His confidence about himself as a father to his children began to return and he was able to recognise his responsibility and the important role he could still play in his children's lives. It was also easier to understand Jenny's angry behaviour as an expression of her need to relate to, and yet to separate from, both parents (see chapter 7 on adolescence). By the time Robin began to feel angry, Frank was ready for that too and was able to make more reasonable arrangements for the children to relate to both parents.

Clarifying repetitive thoughts or images

Another experience which is common after a loss is that of persistent thoughts which simply will not stay away or images which keep returning, unwanted, to the mind's eye. Usually these thoughts and images return with aspects of the loss which still need to be confronted. The counsellor may need to support the client in facing the fear of the thought or image as well as the image itself with its half-hidden message.

Giving information about repetitive thoughts or images

Pat Jones (Table 8.1) in Australia had discovered from the doctor's investigations at his birth that her first-born son Henry was mentally handicapped. About the time of his first birthday she found that she could not get the powerful image of Henry-at-birth out of her mind.

Pat: It's so silly, Henry's *birth* was an easy first delivery. Well, there were no complications and I was able to be wide awake when he was born and Robert was there too, it was wonderful ... but now this picture of Henry still all tiny and wet, but perfectly formed, simply keeps coming back at all times of day and night. I can't keep it away. Am I going mad? Do I need tablets?

Counsellor: This image ... it seems to be linked to an important memory with feelings of...? delight perhaps about your perfectly formed baby?

Pat: (Wistfully) Yes, yes it was delightful. He was so beautiful, so perfect, so tiny, so full of potential. I had *such* dreams for him...

Counsellor: (Carefully) And now?

Pat: (Angrily) *Now*? Now it's so terrible, now my dreams are all gone (breaking down into sobs). Now it's all so awful I can't bear it (sobs deeply for several minutes, gradually the sobbing begins to subside).

Counsellor: Your feelings of pain are completely understandable. You have had a most terrible shock and disappointment. I expect you are wondering how on earth you are going to live with this different Henry now? The image of the original Henry seems to be a bitter reminder of the Henry you have now lost.

Once Pat really began to hear her counsellor's affirmation of her loss she could then take on board the vastness of her loss and all her lost hopes. She was then able to begin the long and often arduous process of grieving for the original Henry she had lost. For Pat this process could well be more difficult being so far from home and support from her family (see Tables 4.1 and 4.2 in chapter 4, and Table 8.1 in chapter 8). Gradually she gained more acceptance of her handicapped son Henry as he truly was. The images then began to disappear.

Pat was able, once her 'image' had been accepted and linked with feelings, to hear the counsellor's 'And now?' for the reality which it represented. She allowed herself to experience her pain at that moment. Other people may not let themselves experience feelings so quickly and it may be useful for the counsellor to invite the client to describe the 'thought' or the 'image' in great detail. If the counsellor can reflect back her picture of the thought or image, linking it tentatively with any feelings she may have perceived, then the client can usually begin to experience the feelings more fully and make sense of the image, sometimes with the counsellor's help.

It is not just adults, but children too, who can be helped to work through their grief. In the next chapter we shall consider ways of working with children who have suffered a loss and with children who have buried their grief. Then in chapters 12 and 13 we shall look at ways of understanding and working with adults who have buried their feelings and whose grief has become more complicated.

SUMMARY

1 If a counselling session is to offer safety and containment it must have clear boundaries. In loss counselling in particular, firm boundaries are important in creating a safe enough place in which to experience feelings.
2 Beginnings are often marked by fear or anxiety and it is useful to offer clear time boundaries and to focus on the feelings the client is experiencing.
3 Endings, both of sessions and of the counselling relationship, may re-evoke feelings associated with loss and separation. These need to be recognised while still holding a firm boundary.
4 Clarity and simplicity of language is useful when trying to clarify and make sense of hallucinations, behaviour, dreams, incorrect beliefs, repetitive thoughts and images. It is also important to recognise the associated feelings.

11

WORKING WITH CHILDREN

There may be fewer children nowadays who lose a parent through death. There are, however, many other circumstantial losses which children need to grieve. A particularly common loss for children is the breakdown of their parents' marriage. In chapter 7 we recognised that children do grieve and that their grief may often be denied by adults in the guise of 'protecting the children'. Children will hide their grief in different ways according to stages in their development and family patterns. However, just as adults can be helped with grieving, as outlined in chapters 9 and 10, so can children. In this chapter we describe ways of working with children who have suffered a loss.

Bowlby observed that if children have had a secure relationship before the loss takes place then the following specific help will enable them to resolve their grief. First they need their questions answered immediately, honestly and factually. Second they need to be allowed and enabled to participate in the family's loss. Last but not least children need a continuing relationship where they can rely on the comforting presence of a parent or another adult. We consider first how this kind of specific help can be given to the reasonably secure child. We then go on to consider some extra help which less secure children may need.

From a child's point of view it would be ideal if his parent(s) could give him the specific help identified by Bowlby. However, this is frequently not available because the adults around a grieving child are usually grieving themselves. Many parents, overwhelmed or embittered by the pain of their own loss, find it hard to be warm, congruent or empathic when feeling so hurt themselves. In addition, the child's reaction can be disturbing and painful and the child's questions, which do need answering, can be infuriating for the hurt adult. This means that other adults, such as relatives, doctors, teachers, priests, friends or counsellors, have an important role to play.

Any adults helping a grieving child need, of course, the basic attitudes and skills described in chapters 2, 9 and 10. This enables a relationship to be built up which the child can rely upon for understanding and comfort.

112

In creating such an environment the adult can also help the child explore her feelings; though it is important to remember that the ease with which a child can identify and give words to feelings depends on her age and her family's attitudes to the expression of feelings. For some children identification of feelings is very difficult and so more direct, active and playful ways of responding need to be found.

IMMEDIACY ABOUT INFORMATION AND FEELINGS

In this section we look at how adults can respond to 'secure enough' children in ways which recognise their specific need to have immediate and honest answers, and which allow them to share in the family grief. Above all else the child needs to know the truth and be responded to warmly and immediately. If the child's feelings or questions are postponed by the adults around, then the child may decide that feelings are unacceptable and push them underground. In this case children may need extra help. We will discuss ways of helping children when this occurs later in this chapter.

In a secure enough setting children will usually try to get the information they need. In chapter 7 we gave an example of how Anne's son Michael used the Polo sweets as a way of questioning Anne about his father's death. When he received an immediate answer that made sense, and had received a cuddle to help recognise and contain the feelings inside him, he was quickly off to play again. That was probably as much grieving as he could do for that moment. However, over the next months he came back again and again to the same questions, as well as asking many others. All his questions needed to be answered straight away and his feelings recognised, often through physical closeness, so that each issue could be resolved and the grief could proceed.

In general it is useful to make physical contact with children who are trying to grieve; not to give false reassurance, to deny feelings, or to change the subject, but to help the child feel safe enough to express and contain the feelings which may be raging inside. As we mentioned earlier children are particularly prone to fantasies or magical thinking which results in their believing they caused a loss. Children need to feel reasonably safe in order to share such fantasies. Only then will they be able to begin to let go of the fantasy and take reality on board.

It may be very difficult for adults, who themselves are grieving, to accept and respond to a child's feelings and questions. This is particularly so when the questions are shocking, critical and hurtful to the parent. It can be tempting to turn the angry or frightened feelings into blame of the other parent, as illustrated in the following anecdote. This can result in the child's sad feelings, evoked for her by this separation from one of the people she loves, being totally ignored.

The Campbell family were going through a difficult time. Peter and Ruth had decided to split up and the children, Philip and Sally, were still rather confused about what was happening. Peter had failed to return Philip's anorak which he had left in Peter's car. It was lashing with rain and they were late for school. Ruth was getting frantic.

Mum: Your Dad's a beast leaving us like this ... he doesn't love us any more!

Philip felt abandoned and confused at this, but his mother suddenly saw his hurt expression and knew it was most important to be able to stop and apologise.

Mum: I'm sorry Philip, I didn't mean that. Of course Dad's not a beast! ... Daddy and I were unable to work things out between us. What I meant was, he doesn't love me any more; but of course he still loves you and Sally and will do always, even if he lives somewhere else.

Philip could then forgive her and was able to make more sense of his situation.

It can often be difficult for divorcing parents to keep the child or children separate from their own angry and bitter feelings. But whatever bitterness exists beween the adults, each ex-spouse continues to be the child's other parent. It is important to recognise and accept the child's own separate feelings about the loss of his or her other parent. To illustrate a way of handling this problem we return to the Campbell family.

Ruth Campbell had tried to help Philip with his own feelings of grief about his father. Although at first he had appeared to accept the separate arrangements, some months later he seemed particularly cross about the timing of visiting arrangements. One day when he was being particularly uncooperative his mother, sensing this was a sign of grief, tried to respond by telling him that both she and his father were concerned about him. She suddenly found Philip shouting 'I hate you. I hate you and I hate Daddy too', rushing to his bedroom and slamming the door. Ruth realised, just, that his onslaught was not personal, and she was able to be patient about his difficult behaviour. Later she was able to talk to him about his angry feelings and his sense of desertion. She had to face many more angry outbursts before his feelings of fury and abandonment were to abate and she could feel reasonably sure that he was not harbouring fantasies of his own guilt. It was important that she treated him consistently with empathy and respect. This was particularly hard for her to do as many people around her, caught up in denial of the child's grief, could only see the child's bad behaviour. They did not understand the importance of listening to his hurt and angry feelings. Fortunately she had one or two good friends who supported her in the long and often excruciatingly lonely task of helping him and Sally through their sad and angry feelings to an acceptance of their loss.

WHEN FEELINGS GET LOST

Unfortunately, in our society, children's feelings about a loss often become buried. Their reactions are then delayed and can turn into complicated behaviour patterns. A child who is helped to grieve will normally have completed the grief work within a year to 18 months. When circumstances are favourable children may be able to work through their grief at about the same rate as adults. However, children who 18 months to 2 years after a loss either show excessive feeling in response to frustrating experiences or who show no signs of distress at all to everyday setbacks, have probably buried their grief and may need extra help to gain access to the 'underground' feelings about the original loss. Children who are less secure themselves, and who have a less secure relationship to a parent or other adult, are more likely to bury grief and to need extra help with their feelings.

As with adults, the feelings most likely to cause difficulty for a child are helplessness, sadness, anger and guilt. This will be particularly so when expression of these feelings has been previously criticised. Returning to Philip and Sally; if in the past Philip's feelings of sadness had led to taunts of 'cry baby' or statements such as 'big boys don't cry', then he might have associated feelings of sadness with vulnerability or helplessness and might try to avoid this by repressing his sadness. If his sister Sally's feelings of anger in the past had brought counterattack or punishment, then she might associate feelings of anger with retribution or even destruction. She might then try to avoid such consequences by repressing her anger and perhaps 'making sense' by deciding she was the 'bad one'.

When working with children whose natural responses to grief have indeed been repressed or cut off in this way, it may be necessary for a helper to use a more direct approach than when working with an adult. An example of this is given in Table 7.1 in chapter 7. Susan was helped to understand more about the meaning of Paul's behaviour. With her new knowledge she was able to ask him directly and clearly about these angry feelings and his misunderstandings. Once his behaviour had been understood as a kind of communication, it was possible to help him understand and express the feelings underlying his behaviour and to give him the information he needed. The difficult behaviour then stopped, he returned to normal development and his self-esteem improved. For Paul, understanding his behaviour helped him to express his true feelings, and grief could proceed.

For some children however, it is very difficult for them to express their feelings. Particular techniques involving play are useful to help such children make more direct contact with their lost feelings. If, to a question about mood or feelings, a child answers 'I don't know', then this could mean something like, 'I don't know about feelings', or 'I don't know how to talk about feelings', or 'I don't know the words...' or 'I just don't want to be bothered at the moment'. At this point some activity which uses methods other than words can be very useful.

Feelings are experienced within the physical body and are also associated with sounds and images. This association offers a wide range of methods to contact feelings in children and then to enable them to express the feelings and begin to unravel the confusion. The following four methods are ones we have found useful. Parents and workers may well already have their own preferred and tested methods.

The 'faces game'

As humans, we express feelings through sound, movement and facial expression. One way to contact a feeling is through known depictions of a 'feeling face'. This visual medium can lead on to further possibilities of expression through sounds, movements and words. Our version of this 'faces game' is based on one described by Claudia Jewett (1984). Another version can be found in a workbook for grieving children written by Marge Heegaard (1988).

The basis of the 'faces game' is to find playful ways to get the child to draw faces showing six different feelings. These are happy, sad, scared, angry, lonely and bored. We have added the bored face to the 'faces game' because children frequently introduce 'bored' as if it were a feeling. It is usually a way of protecting themselves against another more difficult feeling, or else a way of 'not feeling'. Once the faces are drawn they can then be used to help the child identify her feelings or those of adults around her. Sometimes adding sound can free the feeling. The following example illustrates how the 'faces game' can be used.

Use of the 'faces game'

Take a large card and with the child cut it into six equal pieces.
Then:

Adult: Now we're going to make some different faces on the cards – you know how people often tell you what they feel through their faces?

Child: Mmm.

Adult: Do you ever do that?

Child: Don't know.

Adult: Well, let's think about this...
Child: Mmm.
Adult: Supposing your teacher said something like 'It's such a beautiful day I think we should all go to the park and play and have ice-creams'... what might your face look like then?

You might copy the child's face with your face.

Adult: I see, your mouth would go up and your eyes would look 'smiley'. Would you draw that for me?

Offer a piece of card.

Adult: Thank you. Can we find a word to describe that face? Let's write the word underneath the face. Now let's think of another face.

The child may be able to name feelings, demonstrate and draw them. More often their feelings are cut off and they will need some guidance and encouragement.

Adult: What if ... everyone else in your class was taken out to the park and bought ice-creams and you were left to tidy up the classroom?

There are, of course, different feelings that might be expressed in response to this. The feelings could be anger, loneliness, sadness, fear; the expression on the child's face will give you the clues. Help the child explore what feeling is uppermost.

Adult: I see, that certainly looks different. The corners of your mouth would go down.

Imitate the face. Then offer the child a different coloured pencil.

Adult: Perhaps you can draw that face? What sort of face is that?
Child: It's sad.
Adult: Let's write that underneath that face.

If the child has not identified any anger then recognising the 'unfair' nature of this situation may help get in touch with angry feelings. The child may still not relate 'anger' or unfairness to this situation. This may be a clue to you about her difficulty with feeling anger.

Having pictures for two feelings and the words to describe them, you can either give the other 'feeling-words' to write on other cards and then add the faces; or you could describe further situations to evoke the facial expression, then move towards drawing and naming as before. Your choice will depend on such factors as the time available and how easily the child can link a feeling expression to the situation described, also, to some extent, on the knowledge you have of the child's life. Either way you will end up with the six faces looking something like:

HAPPY   SAD   SCARED   ANGRY   LONELY   BORED

As we mentioned earlier children often use 'bored' to describe 'not feeling'. The bored face will need special attention; perhaps the teeth are clenched; perhaps the eyes are closed. Exploring with the child what would happen if the teeth were unclenched, or the eyes opened, and even encouraging the child to clench and unclench her teeth or shut and open her eyes, can lead to a shout of anger or a cry of pain and then sadness.

Once you have the five or six faces on cards there are different ways in which they can be used. Asking the child to choose a card and then talk about the last time she had that feeling or she 'had that face' and affirming the response can help the child recognise the validity of a feeling response to a life situation. She may also be able to use that to grieve. She may, however, avoid certain cards. This is another way of knowing which feelings she is finding hardest. If, for instance, she had difficulty making a sad face and/or a sad drawing (e.g. without tears) and avoided that card, you might begin to focus on that card and as you add the tears say:

Adult: A lot of people I know do this when they are sad. Do you ever look like that?

She may be able to use a sad story or a sad song to help make a sad face. As she comes closer to sad feelings she may want to take another card and make a 'better sad face' or a 'sadder sad face'. It should then be possible to link sad feelings in herself to the loss happening in her life. This technique can also be followed for angry or scared or lonely feelings. In this way the five cards can be used to explore the range of feelings a child is prepared to experience.

One of the uses of the 'faces game' is that it helps identify the feelings a child is avoiding or finding difficult. The problem then is to find other ways to connect and release the feelings. Other media that can be used are sounds, movement, drawing, acting and stories in books, films or on TV.

The use of sound and stories

Stories may enable a child to identify with a person or an animal who is in a similar situation or whose feelings come close to her own. Seeing a child involved with sadness in this way could be the moment to help her into deeper experiencing of that feeling. Examples of story-books that particularly help children are given in Appendix B.

If a child has a problem with sadness, for instance, then making the sound can sometimes connect up the feelings and lead to real experiencing. To do this encourage the child to make a sad noise. If perhaps this is difficult then friendly competition can help with the inhibition.

Adult: I wonder if I can make a sadder sound than you?
            – Do you want to try? (Start softly, working up as she joins in). Waa-a ... louder.

Once her eyes begin to water and she is in touch with real feelings then the 'competition' is over and you have the chance to move into the sharing of real feelings.

The 'boxes game'

Movement can also free feelings. The 'boxes game', again adapted from Jewett (1984), is a movement game which children enjoy.

Have a number of cardboard boxes which can be stacked up on one another to build a 'tower'. You can introduce the game by taking the 'angry card' from the 'faces game' or making an angry face yourself and saying something like:

Helper: Can you copy my face? (Child copies face.)
            Great! Now I wonder what kind of things make you angry?
Child: Don't know.
Helper: Hmmm ... some children I know get angry when things are unfair ... did that ever happen to you?
Child: S'pose so.
Helper: I have a funny game I sometimes play with children when they have those feelings using these boxes. (Take first and largest box). This is for the first unfair thing you can think of ... come on. Give me one.... It's not fair when....
Child: I have to stay in at playtime.
Helper: (Banging down box) I have to stay in at playtime. (Holding second box) And it's not fair when...
Child: I don't get my sweets.
Helper: (Banging second box on top) I don't get my sweets. (Holding third box) And, it's not fair when...
Child: I get the blame.

Helper: (With the next box) And...
Child: It's not fair when Jimmy (his best friend) left for America and
           nobody told me.
and so on.

The helper continues to produce more boxes for each of the child's
known complaints, or the helper's hunches based on what he knows of the
child, or such things as 'other kids tell me it's not fair when they have to go
to bed early ... yes?'

Helper: And now what's fun is to kick them all down, *hard*, like this.

Give a good firm kick so that the boxes really fly around, usually leading
to:
Child: I want a go, me now.

The child may build the tower again on her own in her delight or may
need help. She may need encouragement actually to go at it. Her movements should accompany her words of 'It's not fair when...', thus giving
vent to her anger and real expression to her stored-up resentments.

After a few sessions of such games the child will be more able to express
appropriate emotions to life situations and the behaviour masking the
angry feelings will begin to change. It may be around this time that the
helper or parent can recognise with the child that 'It's not fair when
someone you love goes away' (or dies, or gets taken ill, or whatever fits the
child's situation). These situations may include such things as the child's
best friend leaving the area, the child being hurt or burned and having a
permanent scar or injury, or the child being abused.

If the helper is not the parent and the child's family is one where feelings
are not easily expressed or recognised, it may be important for the child to
tell a parent or parents in your presence 'We were angry today' or for you
to let the parents know this in the child's presence. This helps to legitimise
the child's angry feelings and thus counter the pattern of hiding angry
feelings and creating fantasies of guilt.

The use of art, drama, play and music

Obviously the methods we have already mentioned have an element of
playacting, drawing and sound. These methods are used more extensively
by people trained as art, drama, play and music therapists, with highly
specialised training, to help children (and adults) who have difficulty in
feeling.

WHEN INFORMATION IS LACKING

Some children have considerable confusion over exactly what happened,
when it happened or in what order things happened. Sometimes remem-

bering is too painful and they refuse to remember. Here again particular techniques can be useful, such as making a life-strip or a life-story-book. Both are ways of ordering information and removing confusion. The life-strip is made by taking a long piece of string and pinning on to it, with the child's help, information about herself, photographs of herself, her family, houses she has lived in, people or animals who have died, drawings, maps of journeys, written memories and such like, all dated and in chronological sequence. The life-story-book is similar, with the same sort of information about the child stuck into a scrapbook, again in chronological order. In both cases doing such an activity with the child may enable events and their associated feelings to be recalled and ordered. Starting with 'easier' events can initiate the process, which can then lead on to talking about more 'difficult' events.

FURTHER CONSIDERATIONS

Whatever techniques, methods or resources are used, a child with unresolved grief needs to be enabled to name and really experience the feelings which have been denied. It is then that fantasies and magical thinking are likely to emerge and the adult can supply the information which the child needs. The child may, of course, try to avoid hearing certain items of information but the adult may have to be quite firm about what needs to be done, e.g. 'I know you really don't want to hear about this' or 'I know this gives you really sore feelings but *this is the work we have to do*'.

There are some particularly difficult experiences in the child's life where a child may need specialist help to deal with the effects. Examples of such events are the imprisonment or mental illness of one or both parents or of a sibling, incest in the family, murder of a member of the family or of a friend. The needs of this child are, of course, the same as for any other child experiencing a loss, but the disturbance in the child is likely to be much greater. Therefore the child may well need to get help from workers with specialist training and support, who can offer consistent and committed care to the child, and preferably to the family as well. Continuity at a time of difficult experience is of enormous benefit.

Whatever the loss the child has suffered, her self-esteem will have been damaged and one of the most important healing processes is the repair to self-esteem. Once children begin to express and share their held-in feelings and the grief work begins, then self-esteem will begin to grow. Children also need to be valued for their efforts in coming to terms with their grief and they may need to be helped to learn self-control and responsibility more appropriate to their age.

Children also need to be helped to say 'Goodbye' to the person and sometimes also to the place which is being grieved. For a planned or anticipated loss or separation it is likely to be easier to prepare for the change and say 'Goodbye'. Where this can be done with the real person and the real place, so much the better. If the loss has been sudden and goodbyes have not been said then anniversaries or holidays will often raise this need. If it is not possible to say 'Goodbye' to the person or place, then a symbolic 'Goodbye' using such aids as letters, photographs, drawings and play telephones, will help to fill that gap. These techniques can help to round off the emotional work and enable the child to reinvest in her current life, reconnect with emotions and form satisfying relationships again in the present.

SUMMARY

1 The counselling attitudes are the same when working with children and adults but the skills with children are different in various ways, including a more direct, active and playful style.
2 Children's grief, like adults', requires the expression of feeling and follows a similar pattern. It can be resolved just like adults' grief if certain conditions are met.
3 It is important to respond immediately and openly to children's grief, accepting their feelings whatever they may be.
4 If children's feelings become buried and the reactions delayed, then grief may become complicated and it is sometimes necessary to offer extra help. This help includes encouraging the child to express and share her pent-up feelings, exploring the child's fantasies and magical thinking as well as clarifying facts and realities of the child's life.
5 Specific techniques for working with children can be used in such circumstances.
6 Children will often need extra help to talk about difficult issues such as incest, imprisonment, mental illness.
7 A child's self-esteem will begin to improve as grief gets under way, but help may be needed to affirm her growing self-esteem until she is confident enough to manage with her own resources.
8 Some form of 'Goodbye' usually needs to be said before a child can finish grieving and move on to her current life tasks.

Section IV
COMPLICATED GRIEF

12

UNDERSTANDING GUILT AND ANGER

We indicated in chapter 3 that feelings of both guilt and anger are an essential part of the grieving process. So why introduce them again in this section about complicated grief? We do this not because these feelings are more important than other feelings, nor because they are necessarily the most difficult for the griever or the loss counsellor, but because these feelings are generally experienced as the most powerful. As we mentioned earlier these are the two feelings which people are most likely to fear and repress, and which our society is prone to deny. Thus a collusive secrecy develops between the frightened individual and the denying community which gives particular power to platitudes such as 'Don't speak ill of the dead'. When feelings of guilt and anger are consistently repressed and denied they find expression in very indirect ways and can lead to complications or blocks in the grieving process.

Before looking at ways of working with guilt and anger it is important to understand the origins of guilt.

ORIGINS OF GUILT

In chapter 1 we looked at how our responses to loss are there right from our earliest days. Our first lessons in managing loss happen as we begin to separate from our caring figure, usually our mother.

We suggested that by about the age of 6 months, a baby has begun to have a marked preference for one person who is recognised as different from itself. As this human connection forms, a baby seems to fall in love with that person. This capacity to love is related to the love the baby is receiving. At this stage the loved person is seen as all good.

Over the next 18 months more and more physical and psychological separation takes place. The way these separations take place is very dependent on the quality of attachment to the mother, which in turn is dependent on the mother's personality, her capacity to form attachments and to give care, and the support she is receiving. Simultaneously, as the intense attachment of the early weeks begins to wane and as the baby begins to explore on its own, its mother is beginning to re-engage with her own life and take steps to live more separately from her baby. This means that she is not always available to meet every need and naturally enough the baby hates her for that. It seems to a young child at the stage of infant understanding, that the all-good mother who loves her, is there when needed, cuddles her and holds her tenderly, simply cannot also be the all-bad mother who leaves her, and even chooses to be without her! How could she be? Thus as small children we split up these different feelings, keeping loving feelings in one compartment of the mind and hating and angry feelings in another. In a sense we do not let hateful and angry feelings 'contaminate' good feelings. Perhaps we even fear that hateful feelings could 'eliminate' the loving feelings or, worse still, 'exterminate' the person we also love so much.

Winnicott (1964) suggested that if the mother's failure to be everything the child wants is attuned well enough to the emotional maturity of the child, then this gradual disillusionment will enable personal growth to occur. The combination of this disillusionment in a loving environment where the adults are able to accept and recognise both the toddler's love and hate, enables the child to learn to tolerate some measure of hate towards those she loves. This means that by the time the child is 3 years old she has learned to tolerate both love and hate; in other words ambivalence. In this way the good mother and bad mother will be understood as one 'good-enough mother' rather than two separate mothers.

As well as having an inner mental picture of a 'good-enough' mother, who is not perfect and will fail us, but will also love us, we seem to develop a similar mental picture of ourselves so that we can allow ourselves to be angry and hating as well as loving.

This capacity to love ourselves, including accepting our angry and hating feelings, grows out of our parents' love and acceptance and is the beginning of our self-esteem. Self-esteem is not the only facet of our internal world to be influenced by our parents. Around about the age of 5 we can observe the beginnings of a conscience, which is initially like an internal message system drawn from the external voices of people around us. The external voices are then 'taken inside' this developing conscience, which gives us an internal sense of what is right and wrong, and helps us maintain a good enough picture of ourselves. By about the age of 5 we begin to control our behaviour because of messages from our conscience rather than because of parental commands and the subsequent fear of the loss of their love. Initially these messages are, of course, replicas of the do's and don'ts of our parents. Inevitably therefore where our parents are too strict or unreasonable our conscience will also be too strict. Conversely where parents set no limits on standards of behaviour, a child gets little help in developing her own conscience and is then reliant on learning this from other people, such as teachers, later in her life.

Our conscience communicates with us through a feeling of guilt which we frequently experience physically as a churning in the stomach or as a clutching at the heart. It is sometimes difficult to distinguish guilt from fear. The level of guilt is matched to the demands of the conscience and both grow gradually. When these demands are reasonable then the feeling of guilt is appropriate to the 'naughty' act and we try not to repeat the act.

In our society children are frequently forbidden expression of their angry thoughts, and are often left with guilt not just about unreasonable behaviour, but also about their own feelings and thoughts. Then, rather than being helped to manage their angry behaviour in a context of an understanding of their natural feelings, they are left with unreasonably high levels of guilt. Appropriate levels of guilt about behaviour are difficult to develop when even the thoughts or feelings are not allowed. Feelings of hate in particular are often taboo and denied. Winnicott (1949) pointed out that there are many reasons why a mother might hate her children, yet his list of eighteen reasons for hate caused a furore at the time as the mothers who read Winnicott's words energetically denied their hating feelings! This highlights the difficulty for the child; for if her mother cannot admit to such feelings, how can she possibly learn to express her frightening feelings and manage her difficult behaviour? If, however, a mother can express at least some of her hate, but not act on it, then her child learns to do so as well. She will also be able to tolerate some feelings of hate towards those she loves without having to behave so hatefully that she comes to hate herself. Her self-esteem, which might have been damaged by her hateful behaviour, can be maintained and she can then begin to manage her behaviour.

UNCOMPLICATED ANGER AND GUILT IN GRIEVING

In both Anne's and Geoff's stories in chapter 3 anger and guilt were present; some appropriate, some less appropriate. It is of course appropriate to be angry when we are bereaved or abandoned, yet there is considerable difficulty in acknowledging anger in our society. When asked about their anger, a lot of bereaved will say, 'Of course I'm not angry', yet in the next breath they will express considerable irritation with, for instance, the dead person's employer, or the priest, or the hospital or doctors. This may well be appropriate anger, for mistakes do happen, but frequently such anger, experienced towards someone living, is covering anger which cannot yet be directed towards the dead or lost person, by whom they have been abandoned. This anger is sometimes difficult for the nurse, doctor, priest, or whoever, to manage, but it is quite natural and tends to be short-lived.

Guilt is the other very strong emotion that the grieving feel. Some guilt will be justified, or appropriate, for most of us will be aware of times when we hurt someone we loved and are aware that we can no longer repair or heal the hurt. However, much of the guilt in grief will arise from our difficulty in tolerating our ambivalent feelings of both love and hate towards the lost person. Yes, we did love them, but there were times when we hated them, even wished them dead or at least gone. These thoughts will be the source of some irrational guilt. For even if we have been allowed to express such negative thoughts and feelings as children, we will still feel some guilt when we have similar thoughts as adults. This guilt is natural and brief.

The combination of realistic guilt and unrealistic guilt frequently leads to some idealisation of the dead. Grievers may themselves become aware of the other side to the dead person. Then the idealisation passes quickly and active intervention is not needed. This was illustrated very vividly for a bereavement counsellor leading a group of recently bereaved widows. The following is his account of the session.

'This was my third session with the Smith Street Group. They were all still telling me and each other what wonderful husbands they had lost. What angelic and model husbands they had all been married to! I was just wondering how to confront the group with my disbelief when... "Eeeh ... but my Jimmy, 'e were a reight bugga 'e were!" (God bless you Mrs Roberts!, I thought) ... and then they all started ... and the real husbands began to emerge, human beings every one of them. I was not the only one to feel relief, it surged through the whole group. Mrs Roberts, in expressing the other side of her feelings towards her husband, had helped us all. Each woman in that group was enabled to confront her angry feelings and remember the times she had hated her husband as well as those when she loved him. She could thus take responsibility for her ambivalent feelings. The idealisation, and with it her guilt, began to slip away and she could move towards a more realistic and human "Jimmy" in her own memory and in her heart.'

In the case of idealisation the hating feelings towards the lost person are being denied. The reverse can also happen; rarely in bereavement but commonly in divorce; then the absent person may be vilified and any loving feelings denied. Usually the person who has been left, but also the leaver, has felt very attacked or hurt by the other person. Frequently this hurt has gone unsaid throughout the relationship. This can lead to the griever looking for evidence to make sense of their hurt feelings and indeed asking people to confirm that the lost or dead person was insensitive, difficult, selfish or hateful. In this case the counsellor needs to build a safe enough relationship for the griever or divorcee's hurt to be recognised. As the hurtful aspects of the relationship are recognised and the pain acknowledged and accepted, the griever can then begin to remember the good parts of the relationship and tolerate his or her ambivalent feelings. Where the griever seems to be stuck within the hating aspects of the relationship, the counsellor, in reflecting disbelief in the one-sided portrait being presented, can usually help the griever towards a more realistic picture of the lost person and recognition of the ambivalent feelings. This then enables inappropriate guilt to lift and the grief work to continue.

Thus the anger and guilt are linked to coming to terms with a real relationship with the lost person and also with the ambivalent feelings towards the person who has gone. A major part of work with the grieving is, therefore, to help them explore the relationship through working with the feelings at the edge of awareness. With such an exploration of these (sometimes difficult) feelings, the positive and negative aspects of the lost person can be discussed and a more realistic picture created. With this more balanced and realistic memory it is paradoxically more possible to let go of the lost relationship. This is as true for divorce and other losses as it is for bereavement.

We have outlined above some of the ways of working with the natural anger and guilt experienced in the average grief process. Such difficulties with anger and guilt are usually short-lived and, once recognised, the feelings begin to wane and grief moves on. However, when nothing seems to move and a particular feeling seems to be well and truly stuck, then it is likely we are working with complicated anger and guilt.

COMPLICATED ANGER AND GUILT IN GRIEVING

In chapter 4 we looked at how the outcome of grief was markedly affected by external and internal determinants. With this knowledge we are alert to the circumstances where grieving is more likely to be prolonged and complicated. Certain external circumstances, such as coincidental deaths or losses and successive deaths and losses, result in a more prolonged grief, but not necessarily a complicated grief. If the person has developed the capacity to grieve they will eventually manage even the most extreme external circumstances. However, if this capacity has not developed or barely developed, then whatever the external determinants the grieving can become complicated with the griever stuck in one phase or with one particular set of feelings. Without fail the two emotions that are particularly difficult to manage in complicated grief are anger and guilt. In other words it is the inability to deal with ambivalent feelings, or to tolerate hate within a loving relationship, which is critical; critical both during the relationship as well as after the end of the relationship.

We suggested earlier in this chapter that the ability to tolerate ambivalent feelings develops during the first three years of life. However, some children are not given much help in learning to tolerate ambivalence. When a child is not allowed or enabled to have hating feelings towards those she loves, then she 'cannot' be angry with them or hate them. In the child's logic: if she cannot hate her mother at all, then the mother must be 'nothing-but-good'; and if mother is 'nothing-but-good', she, the child, must be 'nothing-but-bad' to have these 'bad' feelings; if she is 'all-bad' then she must deserve to be hated and punished and must therefore be guilty: a very tortuous train of thought! It will then be difficult for her to love herself and her self-esteem will not be able to grow. When the capacity to express anger is blocked and guilt is overwhelming, then the ability to differentiate between appropriate and inappropriate guilt is low. The capacity to repair and forgive is limited and self-esteem will be further damaged. Guilt will be the predominant experience and losses in adult life will be difficult to grieve. Patterns of particular behaviour or feelings then develop, which protect the griever from other unwanted or intolerable feeling, but which prevent the grief work from continuing. Some of the patterns which protect a person from difficulties with guilt and anger will be outlined below. When these patterns of idealisation, bitterness, depression, or of strong suicidal urges develop and persist, it is important to recognise how they protect and why they are needed.

Idealisation is one way of protecting the self from difficulties with hate and anger in a relationship. The Smith Street Group offered an example of brief idealisation, which quickly disappeared when Mrs Roberts admitted to feelings of hate and enabled the others to do likewise. In complicated grief, however, the idealisation pattern seems to get completely stuck. The relationship is regarded as 'perfect' with a total denial of natural anger, hurts or disagreements. This can happen between couples in a relationship but also between parents and their children. When one member of the relationship is lost, then a persistent inability to tolerate hateful and angry feelings results in prolonged idealisation which often becomes stuck. A common sign of this is the creation of a permanent 'shrine'. The shrine is sometimes the dead person's room or it may be the corner of a room set out with pictures and flowers or may include the urn containing the ashes.

Prolonged idealisation can also occur when difficult losses happen to people who already have severe difficulty in expressing feelings. Imagine, for instance, the situation of parents who have difficulty in expressing anger constructively having an unresolved row with their teenage son. He then rushes out of the house, takes the family car and is killed in an accident. The parents' feelings of guilt and responsibility may be so immense and inexpressible that they lead to idealisation and then the creation of a permanent shrine.

Another fraught situation for people who have difficulty in expressing feelings, and who deny anger and hate, is the long-term nursing of a relative. The survivor may well have hated the relative at times in the past, particularly if they had nursed the relative out of a sense of duty and if they had been hurt when the relative had become spiteful as they aged. If the nursing person was unable to speak of this hurt or to recognise and express their hate, then when the death actually occurs, naturally enough the hurt and hate predominate. This can become entrenched and the griever gets stuck with a bitterness that almost matches the spitefulness of the departed person, thus leading to more hate. Any feelings of sadness and love have become lost. The bitterness seems to prevent any feelings of love, and the griever seems wrapped in the pain of bitterness rather than the pain of grief.

Prolonged depression may be another protective pattern. Natural feelings of anger associated with grief in some people with damaged self-esteem are often turned against the self and experienced as guilt. Such inappropriate guilt feelings thus exacerbate the natural guilt feelings associated with loss. This double guilt is intolerable for some people and can lead to a cutting off of not just all angry and hateful feelings, but of feelings altogether. Such lack of feeling may be experienced as depression for the client but may only be experienced as confusion or blankness by the counsellor. The counsellor may in some sense be 'protected' from the awfulness of the client's depression. The client therefore remains out of touch and this pattern, like the others, may get quite stuck. Similarly for adult survivors of childhood sexual abuse, the naturally occurring loss of adolescence may evoke strong feelings of inexpressible anger and helplessness about earlier losses. These losses such as loss of innocence, loss of self-esteem, loss of normal peer relationships, loss of the ability to play, loss of safety and protection and loss of trust, remain unnoticed and the survivor is overwhelmed by feelings of guilt. Prolonged depression may follow unless help is given.

Depression, although protecting the person from even less tolerable feelings of guilt or helplessness, may in itself be an intolerable experience. Because it is uncomfortable for others too, the depressed person may find themselves very isolated and alone. This can sometimes lead to suicide seeming to be the only possible response to loss or bereavement. Although suicide may have a number of different psychological roots, it too can often be understood as anger turned against the self or despair about ever being free of the burden of guilt. Those who do commit suicide after a loss will have done so for a variety of reasons and different meanings can be attributed to it. An elderly person who found it impossible to grieve the death of his wife might see suicide as the only way of holding on to her and rejoining her. Someone else overwhelmed by feelings of numbness and despair or by intense feelings of survivor guilt from long ago, might eventually find it impossible to go on living with these feelings. Another person might consider that the intensely angry and revengeful feelings felt in response to a current loss could only be expressed through the revenge of suicide. And yet another might decide that the only expression for overwhelming guilt feelings would be the most severe punishment imaginable to themselves; their own killing. Whatever the reason or meanings of the act, suicide as a response to loss usually grows out of a sense in that person that their feeling-world cannot be adequately understood by anyone else.

Often low self-esteem and feelings of hopelessness or helplessness contribute to this position. In chapter 13 we consider ways of working with those who have suicidal thoughts or intentions and consider the extra support that should be given in supervision for those whose clients attempt or succeed in committing suicide.

Another protective pattern with some similarity to suicide is that of self-inflicted hurt such as wrist-slashing, biting or scratching oneself and head-banging. These acts seem to function as a way of both giving some expression to despair and hopelessness as well as giving some protection from really experiencing the feelings. The physical pain for some people seems to function as a way of dulling the psychic pain of despair. Unfortunately those around them do not necessarily hear this message. They may respond with anger and punishment, probably causing the person to withdraw further and to feel even more hopeless about ever being heard or understood.

In all these instances the task of the loss counsellor is to help the griever explore all aspects of the relationship with the lost person, including the painful areas being avoided. In this way the resentments, frustrations and hates, along with the loving feelings, can be recognised and accepted. In the next chapter we discuss ways of working with the apparently intolerable feelings of guilt and anger.

SUMMARY

1 Guilt and anger are the feelings which most people are likely to fear and repress and which our society is most likely to deny.

2 From well before 6 months babies begin to separate from, and have feelings about, their mothers.

3 There seems to be a tendency in this separation process to split the all-good-and-all-loving feelings from all-bad-and-all-hating feelings.

4 When a mother can manage very gradually to fail to meet the infant's needs at a pace that is attuned to that infant, then the infant will be able to understand that the 'good mother' she loves and the 'bad mother' she hates are one and the same person.

5 This 'good enough' mother enables the child, by about the age of 3, to tolerate love and hate towards the same person.

6 Around the age of 5 the child begins to develop a conscience of her own and a consequent capacity to feel guilt about her actions.

7 When guilt is appropriate to an act then it can be listened to, responded to and the wrongs put right. Appropriate guilt can lead to reparation and forgiveness and the child can feel good about herself again.

8 When angry and hateful feelings have been denied in childhood, then

those adults will fail in a crisis to distinguish between thoughts and feelings on the one hand and action or behaviour on the other hand. In a crisis such as loss, they may build up an inappropriate burden of guilt about both thoughts and feelings. This actually hinders them from moving through the grief process towards a letting go of that which is lost.

9 In complicated grief, when ambivalence cannot be tolerated and guilt is excessive, protective patterns develop and grief fails to progress. Feelings are further denied.

10 Those who have severe difficulty in tolerating feelings of anger or hate towards those they have lost develop a protective pattern of idealisation which will protect them from unbearable guilt.

11 When they have severe difficulty in recognising feelings of love and compassion towards those they have come to hate, they may protect themselves from unbearable pain through vilification.

12 Denial of all feelings may lead to persistent depression.

13 Suicide may be a result of anger or guilt turned against the self together with a conviction that no one can understand or tolerate their unbearable feelings.

13

WORKING WITH GUILT AND ANGER IN COMPLICATED GRIEF

In the last chapter we described how complicated grief arises. Complicated grief may be difficult to work with and the counsellor needs to have developed self-knowledge and have integrated the basic counselling attitudes outlined in chapter 2, so that when sudden difficulties with acceptance, empathy and congruence occur they are recognised as uncharacteristic. If a counsellor realises that she is unexpectedly angry, puzzled, disbelieving or judgemental, then this will lead her to reflect. Is she picking up the client's difficulties with anger and guilt? Or has the client's material sparked off feelings associated with unresolved losses of her own? In chapter 15 we consider how a supervisor can help a counsellor handle situations where her grief is interfering with her work as a counsellor.

This awareness of the counsellor that the anger or guilt which she is sensing 'does not belong to her' is a very important advanced counselling skill. It enables the counsellor to recognise that she is sensing the frightening feelings behind the protective patterns that develop in complicated grief. When feelings of anger and guilt are too frightening they are avoided or denied and a protective pattern develops (see chapter 12). This avoids feelings of guilt and anger but also prevents the grief work from progressing. The capacity of the counsellor to pick up an underlying feeling is, of course, one aspect of sensitivity which requires continued commitment to developing self-awareness. A decision to use such awareness in counselling often grows over a period and arises out of a series of interactions. Thus such responses are usually very specific to those two people at that point in the relationship. This makes it difficult to give brief or useful vignettes, and the examples given here need to be understood as greatly simplified parts of a much more complex whole relationship. The counsellor has to decide at what point in the relationship to use this sensing of the underlying feelings to help the client. The client may be desperately trying not to experience a feeling which, however, needs to be addressed if the grief process is to proceed. The counsellor's skill is to recognise and understand the protective mechanism and its function, without losing sight or sense of the avoided feeling. In this way the client can begin to feel safe enough to recognise and accept the feeling, trusting that the counsellor will not be overwhelmed by such a dreaded feeling and thereby learning that he too can manage the feeling.

There are many patterns of behaviour which people use in everyday life to protect themselves from other more frightening feelings, which are either inconvenient or unpleasant to experience. In ordinary grief the strong feelings in response to loss tend to break through any loosely held protective patterns. Where, however, the capacity to grieve is limited, then the protective patterns will be held much more firmly and the counsellor will probably find this kind of grief reaction much more challenging to work with. In considering the following examples of such 'stuck' patterns we shall:

1 Outline the protective mechanism with an illustrative example;
2 Consider the function of the protective pattern;
3 Consider the counsellor's likely feelings and possible dilemmas;
4 Suggest some possible strategies and verbal responses;
5 Consider common counsellor difficulties associated with this pattern.

THE PATTERNS

1 Idealisation as a protection against anger or guilt: Mrs Brown

Mrs Roberts from chapter 12 helped the other widows to remember their more real husbands through her acceptance of her own angry feelings with her husband Jimmy. Their idealisations of their husbands were short-lived. When, however, 'unacceptable' angry feelings get 'stuck' as they did for Mrs Brown then the idealisation pattern becomes more engrained.

Mrs Brown, an elderly and highly dependent widow, has talked nonstop about her dead husband Michael, who had gone off fishing against her will on a very stormy day and been drowned.

Mrs Brown:　He was so wonderful, he was the most perfect husband anyone could ever wish for. There was never an angry word between us... He looked after me, cared for me, did the garden, even helped old Mrs Jones next door. We loved each other so much, there was nothing ever came between us...

How the pattern functions

Mrs Brown seems here to be protecting herself from any feelings of anger in response to loss. Her anger may be greatly intensified by her additional angry feelings about his going off fishing that day and leaving her alone. His leaving her alone turned out to be not just that Wednesday but for ever, and her anger in response to this fate must have seemed unmanageable to Mrs Brown. To cope, she has denied her anger and covered it over with idealisation. Her grief is stuck.

Counsellor's feelings and dilemmas

The counsellor listening to Mrs Brown might feel some surprise at this paragon of all human virtue and is then likely to feel some irritation as the eulogy continues and the more complete picture is not recognised. He might be wistfully remembering Mrs Roberts from the Smith Street Group who had been able to let go of her idealised Jimmy quite quickly, to everyone's relief. How might the counsellor use this irritation constructively?

Unfortunately tackling Mrs Brown's idealisation head on might only serve to convince her that her angry feelings really were unacceptable or even dangerous. On the other hand, going along with the idealisation of Michael will almost certainly convince Mrs Brown that even her counsellor is frightened by her angry feelings; they must indeed be dangerous!

Counsellor's responses

Somehow the counsellor needs to find a way of highlighting the pattern, recognising its protective function and recognising what is being guarded against: in this case feelings of anger. If the counsellor can actually name, make sense of, and show an accepting understanding of these 'dangerous' angry feelings, then they are already less dangerous and becoming more recognised. The following counsellor response is just one attempt to combine these elements.

'I get a sense from you, Mrs Brown, that Mr Brown was ... well ... a bit of a saint really ... almost not quite human. I'm thinking that it might be a bit awkward to be cross with a saint?... Yet I guess you could have felt quite cross when he left without you that morning.'

Perhaps you can think of other responses which combine these elements and help to make sense of the protective pattern?

Counsellor's difficulties

Counsellor difficulties associated with this pattern can be the pressure to collude with the idealisation of her husband, Michael, or the temptation to be irritable with this 'ridiculous' picture. A further source of potential irritation might be Mrs Brown's ability to ignore the counsellor's intervention which might make it necessary to repeat this response on several occasions. It may then be necessary to recognise with her how she refuses to hear certain things. A possible intervention might be:

> 'Mrs Brown, I notice that every time I raise the possibility of having angry feelings about Michael or Michael's death you seem not to hear me. I guess there's been something really scary about that. Yet I wonder if we could look at that now?'

It may take some time before there is enough trust for the client to begin to face the cut-off feelings. Discussion with a supervisor should help the counsellor to steer the path between collusion and too rapid confrontation.

2 Vilification as a protection against pain and underlying love: Frank

Some vilification is also natural as a part of the response to loss and may indeed be indistinguishable from the initial expression of anger at having been abandoned. When, however, the vilification gets stuck with repeated condemnations it may be to protect the griever from extreme feelings of pain related to the lost love.

Frank (Table 8.1) is talking about his wife Lizzie 6 months after they separated. His tone is clipped and spiteful.

Frank: Lizzie was so useless. I was forced to marry her because she threatened to kill herself and the baby if I didn't. She was depressed all the time and never did anything in the house, the place was a tip. Now she won't talk to me and everything goes through my sister Mary. She's trying to get Mary on her side ... she's spiteful, cunning and stupid and can't even manage the children.

How the pattern functions

By this time Frank seems bitter, has not got a good word to say about Lizzie or the children and seems to be protecting himself against any feelings of pain and sadness he would have to feel, if he could recognise his love for them. The more bitter and accusatory he becomes with them, the more Lizzie and the children withdraw from him, thus reinforcing his sense of bitterness and loneliness. His grief is stuck.

Counsellor's feelings and dilemmas

The counsellor listening to Frank might initially feel fed up with his bitter haranguing and find herself wanting to punish him for being so arrogant and so beastly about Lizzie. Or she might find herself drawn into the anti-Lizzie vilification campaign and find herself thinking that Lizzie ought to 'pull up her socks' or improve in some way. Either way she is getting drawn into the accusatory pattern and, like Frank himself, is losing touch with Frank's internal world. How might she recognise or confront Frank's protective strategy without being drawn into the accusatory pattern and being punitive in her responses?

Counsellor's responses

The challenge to the counsellor is to recognise the existence and value of Frank's internal world of hidden feelings, while also making sense of the protective pattern and not punishing him. The following two responses attempt, in slightly different ways, to combine these elements.

> 'At the moment, Frank, you seem to be seeing Lizzie as "all-bad". I'm wondering whether seeing her as nothing-but-bad is in some way protecting you from actually experiencing how hurt you have been by the Lizzie you love(d).'
> OR
> 'Frank: I'm guessing that deep inside you are feeling real sadness and pain for the love which has been lost. Seeing Lizzie as "all-bad" or hating Lizzie may be protecting you from actually experiencing those unbearable feelings of longing and pain.'

Perhaps you can think of other ways of challenging Frank's pattern without being punitive? Obviously a non-punitive tone of voice is also essential.

Counsellor's difficulties

There are, of course, times when any words we use may be heard as punitive by certain clients. These situations are always worth discussing with a supervisor to help check whether the 'being-punished' feelings in the client are actually coming from the client's internal emotional world, or are indeed an appropriate response to inappropriately punitive or clumsy remarks made by the counsellor.

It is easy for the counsellor to forget that these unpleasant vilification patterns in the client often cover up deep-seated fear and pain. Rather like a hedgehog or cactus, the prickly bits are there to protect the more vulnerable parts underneath.

3 Anger as a protection against intimacy and underlying despair: Christopher

When a trust has been betrayed and an intense intimacy lost, then the world

138

may seem to contain only helplessness and despair. To begin to trust anyone else might seem to be courting further rejection. Ferocious anger may be a way of protecting a person from beginning to build a new trust or from feelings of helplessness or despair. They can therefore find themselves avoiding the very closeness or trust they need to help with the grief. Sometimes they can swing between the two positions of cautious approach and then vehement avoidance, tinged with longing.

Christopher (Exercise 9.3) talks of his lover Jake who recently died of Aids. He is angry and isolated and is very frightened of trusting the counsellor. He walks into the first session shouting.

Christopher: Just how do you think you can help me? Do you know what it feels like to have your lover die? You can't give him back to me, can you?

How the pattern functions

Christopher has been deeply hurt and also frightened by Jake's death. Reactions of blame he has met with in society, and to a lesser extent in his own family, have not helped him with the inappropriate guilt he has experienced in relation to Jake's illness. Some of their gay friends helped enormously while Jake was ill and dying, but they now seem to have drifted away. Christopher is alone in his grief and is very frightened of trusting anyone, especially anyone outside his immediate circle, whom he fears might reject him. Yet he desperately needs someone with whom to share his grief. Anger is often an expression of some kind of hope of involvement; it can also serve to keep someone at arm's length. This is potentially confusing to the unwary counsellor!

Counsellor's feelings and dilemmas

The counsellor faced with Christopher's angry outburst might first be tempted to ignore the anger and work to reassure or calm him down and then to feel very sorry for him, the victim. Or she might be tempted to retaliate and fiercely insist that he stop being angry or even suggest that he 'pull himself together'. She might even find herself drawn into the pattern of dread surrounding Aids.

Counsellor's responses

The counsellor's challenge is not to flinch or to be controlled by Christopher's anger, but to try to recognise its various messages without retaliation, punishment or dread. It is important to be direct and not to 'beat about the bush', nor to use euphemisms. Society's various unrealistic attitudes to Aids make all of this difficult. However, the basic counselling approach of recognising feelings and trying to understand the meaning of behaviours still applies. The following responses attempt to initiate this process of recognition and unravelling, which could lead to the sort of trust and intimacy which Christopher both longs for and fears.

> 'That's right, Christopher, I can't give Jake back to you and, you're right, I don't know what it feels like for you. I guess you feel pretty furious about everything and are not at all sure you can trust a stranger like me at this point?'
> OR
> 'Christopher, you are really angry right now and that certainly makes sense when you have been so let down. I imagine you might be very wary about trusting me in case I let you down too?'

Can you now think up other words which could help Christopher to explore his angry feelings and understand more about his dilemma of longing for intimacy and yet fearing rejection? This struggle with trust can cause great loneliness.

Christopher's pattern has some similarities to the previous pattern of vilification illustrated by Frank. There are differences; Frank was protecting himself from feelings of pain and underlying love, and was grieving a relationship which had been broken, but the person was still alive. Christopher was trying to protect himself from his dilemma of a longing for intimacy and yet his fear of rejection, as well as from his underlying feelings of loneliness and despair. Here the counsellor inevitably challenges both Christopher's dilemma and his loneliness. It is important that the counsellor recognises this.

Counsellor's difficulties

Again it is important for the counsellor to respond neither defensively nor in a punishing way. Recognising the shared responsibility for the relationship can help to take any pity or condescension out of the response. Tone of voice, pacing and body language will also influence the sense of 'equality' in the relationship.

4 Depression as a protection against feelings: Martha and Peter

Depression can protect some people from feelings of unbearable anger and hate by cutting off feeling altogether. Sometimes the depression manifests itself as a vague sense of hopelessness (Martha) or it may be experienced as a total blankness (Peter). Neither of these 'protections' can really protect anyone from feeling absolutely dreadful. Prolonged depression in response to loss may be a long tunnel of darkness, hopelessness and sometimes utter despair. It was like this for Martha.

Martha

Martha shuffled in looking grey, drooping and without any sparkle of life. Her boyfriend, Tim, had committed suicide in September last year. He killed himself using his car exhaust. It is now February and she has so far shown no signs of grieving, but is stuck in a deep feelingless depression. She does not mention Tim.

> Martha: Well, it's all right really. I'm just depressed, that's all. I left my job in November, because I wasn't much use at it anyway... I don't feel like bothering to go for anything else... What's the point?... It's all hopeless.

How the pattern functions

Martha learnt long ago that anger and hate were unacceptable feelings to the adults who cared for her. Therefore after Tim's death she could not feel anger nor hate him for what he had done. Had she done so she would have been overwhelmed by guilt, so cut feelings off instead and adopted the protective pattern of despair expressed through hopelessness.

Counsellor's feelings and dilemmas

The very 'feeling-less-ness' of depression can be hard for the counsellor to bear and he may find himself feeling helpless. A common counsellor response to feelings of helplessness is to set off on a wild goose chase to 'find-the-feeling'. The client is by now, of course, adept at hiding feelings and will reject any help that is likely to evoke feelings, so she can draw the counsellor into just such a chase. This can often be a very intellectual exploration. The overall result is to distance both of them even further from the actual experiencing of the feelings of helplessness. The counsellor needs to be very careful not to be drawn into doing 'all the work'. A simple rule-of-thumb for a counsellor is that when he finds himself doing more than half the work then he should ask himself what is going on. It may be that the counsellor needs to face feelings of hopelessness and helplessness in himself in order to stay with, and truly empathise with, Martha's state rather than 'running away' into being clever.

What can also happen when depression protects a client from anger and guilt is that the counsellor can find himself actually experiencing either helplessness, anger or guilt and sometimes all three together. Having checked with himself that these feelings are in no way his own, the counsellor has to decide how to bring these lost feelings into the open. Again a way has to be found which is not punitive.

Counsellor's responses

As with other protective patterns the main strategy is to recognise the pattern and the underlying feelings. This gradual (and it is often very gradual) recognition, expression and acceptance of anger and resentment usually results in the guilt beginning to lift and with it the depression lightens. The counsellor's response below includes mention of Tim even though Martha avoids any mention of his name or his suicide. The counsellor also uses his own sense of anger as the basis for the suggestion that Martha may be feeling this about Tim.

'Martha, I notice you don't mention Tim or how he died. Perhaps you're not sure it's O. K. to mention him? Perhaps you're also not sure that you are allowed to be angry about him and what he did?'

It is common for depressed clients to be particularly resistant to recognising and accepting the underlying feelings, so it may be necessary to comment on this. The following are examples of such responses.

'I notice, Martha, that when I raise the possibility of your having any feelings you seem not to hear what I'm saying.'
OR
'Martha, I find it interesting that when I mention Tim there seems to be no reaction from you. It's almost as if you didn't know or didn't dare to know whom or what I was talking about.'

Counsellor's difficulties

Working with depression is challenging and often requires enormous patience. Counsellors should keep taking such work to supervision. The supervisor can then help to decide when a depression is so well and truly stuck that referral to someone more specialised is necessary. Referral procedures and supervision are discussed in chapters 14 and 15 respectively.

Peter
We mentioned earlier that depression can also manifest itself as blankness. This is how Peter in the following example reacted to loss. Again the difficult feelings are usually anger and hate but blankness may also be hiding extreme feelings of pain and loss.

Peter limped in bravely, trying to look cheerful, and yet looking curiously bland and unreal. He had been a sports teacher and an outstanding all-round sportsman. When he was 24 he was involved in a climbing accident in Glencoe and had had to have one of his legs amputated. His physical recovery from the amputation had been continually dogged by pain from his missing leg. He was referred for counselling by his doctor who noticed that Peter was having unexpected difficulties in managing his prosthesis.

Peter: (Blank voice with little expression) I really am much better now, the doctor's been awfully helpful. I'm most grateful... They've given me a special car now, you know, as well ... and I can more or less get about, ... not as far as Glencoe of course... (looks slightly surprised)...

How the pattern functions

Peter seems to be protecting himself from extreme feelings of anger about the accident and his helplessness about his current condition and situation. His previous identity and sense of himself had been that of an extremely able-bodied person. The challenge of managing a prosthesis and adapting to his new identity was proving more than he could bear. However, like Martha he had learned that anger and hate were unacceptable feelings, so he responded by cutting off all feelings about himself or his situation; except that the word 'Glencoe' slipped out.

Counsellor's feelings and dilemmas

The counsellor might feel intense sympathy with Peter's difficult situation and would realise that he would have to draw on every bit of his maturity to manage his new life. Yet she might find herself curiously absent and uninvolved as she heard his string of words, perhaps only coming alive when Peter mentions 'Glencoe'. How might she use this oblique mention of Glencoe to help Peter get in touch with his painful feelings?

Counsellor's responses

As with Martha the counsellor would have to make choices about which aspect of the protective pattern to highlight and which of the underlying feelings to mention. She might also find her responses unheard.

'Peter, you seemed almost surprised just now when you found yourself mentioning Glencoe. I'm guessing that there is still an enormous number of painful memories associated with Glencoe and the amputation of your leg.'
OR
'Your words, Peter, don't seem to have much meaning for me right now... and yet I'm aware that the words may be protecting you from some uncomfortable feelings underneath. I heard the word "Glencoe"...?'

Counsellor's difficulties

The counsellor's difficulties would be similar to those of Martha's counsellor. The counsellor might find herself drawn into discussions about climbing or prostheses. She might need to reflect on how well Peter was managing to avoid his painful feelings.

5 Suicidal thoughts as a fantasy of release from pain and despair: Vilna

Suicidal thoughts in response to loss, whatever the situation, usually grow out of a sense in that person that their feeling-world cannot be understood by anybody else. Often low self-esteem and feelings of hopelessness, helplessness or powerlessness contribute to this position. Sometimes clients mention the word 'suicide' as a way of expressing feelings of despair which, when expressed and recognised, may lift. Others may or may not mention suicide, but their intense feelings of despair may be leading them to think about ways of ending their life as the only apparent way of ending their despair. This was Vilna's position.

> Vilna had been abused both physically and sexually as a child by her own father. Her younger brother Stefan had, as he grew older, become her protector and her best friend. Eventually the abuse had stopped. Stefan had recently married, however, and his young wife, who was very jealous of the relationship between him and Vilna, was encouraging him to emigrate to America to join her family. Vilna felt sure that they would go and that she would be left alone in Britain to look after her widowed father, who was becoming increasingly infirm and dependant. The rest of her family still lived in Czechoslovakia.

Vilna: If Stefan goes, I can see no hope for me. Father will have to come and live with me and I will think only of the past and there will be no one to protect me. Why should I go on living?

Some weeks later.

Vilna: They have gone. I'm all alone, he has moved in and although he can't hurt me any more I can remember only the past. There is no one to protect me now and I can't see why I should go on...

How the pattern functions

Vilna seems to see suicide as a way out of her despair, as a way of escaping from her apparently impossible situation and of not feeling her painful and 'unacceptable' feelings. In a sense her ideas about suicide are a 'comfort' to Vilna in her despair. She will need enormous courage to face these feelings and deal with the situation. She will need to trust her counsellor to stay with her through all these difficulties, so that her feelings of abandonment can be expressed and trust begin to grow again. It is not clear whether she can manage that. Her counsellor is a woman and the other woman in Vilna's life, her mother, was unable to protect her. Her mother had abandoned her to her father during her life and had now seemed to have done so again through her death. Could Vilna muster the courage to trust another woman? She certainly did not feel she could trust a man and for this reason had sought a woman as counsellor.

Counsellor's feelings and dilemmas

The feelings which the client cannot or dare not express may be felt quite intensely by the counsellor. As with other patterns the counsellor will need great sensitivity to know when to introduce the client to these 'unfelt' feelings. Without this sensitivity trust cannot be built. Such trust takes time to build, but it needs to exist before the client can begin to express despair and the underlying anger in words rather than in acts.

The counsellor may experience the 'instinct to save life' when working with someone considering suicide. Human instinct is to save life. Just think of the foolhardy things people do in an emergency to save life! The counsellor may need help from her supervisor to contain this instinct and recognise her fear of the suicidal act itself. Containment of her own fear should enable her to recognise more fully the client's probable feelings of intense pain or despair and hopelessness, along with low self-esteem. These feelings may be masking more deep-seated feelings of anger or hate.

Another strong feeling the counsellor may experience is her own loss of hope, especially if the client seems to give up hope altogether. It is important for the counsellor to hold on to her own sense of hope, while recognising the client's hopeless feelings. If the counsellor found herself struggling with 'hope' in such a situation, it would be essential to take these feelings to supervision. It may also be useful for the counsellor to reflect to the client the possibility that she is holding some unconscious hope for the client, until the client is ready to take it back.

Counsellor's responses

Again in her response the counsellor needs to recognise the different feelings from which the client is protecting herself. These various feelings seem to come in layers. The counsellor's experience as well as the client's has been compared to lasagne, with layer upon layer of different ingredients. Sometimes the 'crust' of despair can seem as impenetrable as over-baked lasagne and sometimes the underlying anger can spurt up and hit us in the face; just like the tomato sauce if we push through the top layer too vehemently!

It is important for the counsellor to go firmly but gently, gradually letting the layer of despair melt and the underlying feelings emerge in their own time. This firmly-but-gently approach can be expressed through a firm and regular commitment of time with a clear ending as outlined in chapter 10 and with a consistent refocusing on the top feeling layer. The following is a counsellor's possible response to Vilna's second statement.

> 'You don't seem to see any other way out of your situation at the moment than to consider suicide. Your despair must be enormous for you to come to this conclusion. I wonder if it feels as if there is no one who could even begin to understand your despair?'

Perhaps you could formulate a possible response to Vilna's first statement?

Counsellor's difficulties

It is important for the counsellor to remember that although attitudes towards suicide in the west have become less punitive in the course of this century, some religious groups do have strongly disapproving views. Counsellors need to be aware of these differences and look out for punitive attitudes in the clients and/or in their close friends and family. Other groups, especially those who believe in reincarnation, are less likely to see suicide as a way out of despair.

Some of the major counsellor difficulties which arise when working with clients experiencing suicidal thoughts and wishes have already been mentioned. In hearing clients talk of suicide there are two main sources of difficulty. First the counsellor has to live with the fear that the client may indeed commit suicide. Second, if the counsellor has had experience of suicide in her life, either through her own experiences of persistent suicidal thoughts or through the suicide of someone close, then she will find the threat of suicide difficult to bear.

If a suicide does actually occur, whether threatened or not, then the counsellor will need care from colleagues and supervisor. She too has suffered a loss and may suffer from severe feelings of guilt, failure and possibly loss of self-esteem. It is wise to have extra supervision at such a time to receive the understanding and support that this relationship should give.

FURTHER COUNSELLOR DILEMMAS WHEN WORKING WITH COMPLICATED GRIEF

Apart from the difficulties which have already been highlighted arising when working with complicated grief, there are other dilemmas that the counsellor may need to address. We shall consider dilemmas associated with how to respond to silence; how to respond to clients arriving late for sessions; if you are medically qualified, when to prescribe drugs to counteract the depression; how to manage grieving clients if you have to change job or move away.

Silence

A basic counsellor dilemma arises over silence. It may be difficult to tell whether a particular silence is a comfortable, even intimate, sharing of silent time together, or is a primitive or frightened non-responding. Generally that difference is clear and when it is not, we can usually explore the nature of the silence with the client.

However, for clients experiencing depression even the gentlest of explorations of the silence itself can sometimes seem like an invasion into the very world being protected. The counsellor may need extraordinary patience, as well as firmness of boundaries, to offer the quality of safety the client needs in order to begin to experience a feeling.

Lateness

Missing sessions, arriving late or forgetting to pay (if this is relevant) are common enough behaviours when clients are working through complicated grief. They can all be seen as communications to the counsellor. There is a stage when anger begins to break through the protection of depression. Because the anger is still largely unconscious, it is hard for the client to bring the anger into the session as a conscious feeling or experience. The anger therefore may find its way into behaviour-as-communication (sometimes called acting out) and manifest itself as missing sessions, coming late or forgetting to pay. Whilst it is enormously important that the counsellor notice this behaviour, it is also important that the client is not punished. One possible counsellor response to a client who is late for a session which incorporates these features is:

> 'Yes, sure you're 10 minutes late. *I'm* not particularly worried by or interested in the lateness itself. After all it's your time ... but I am interested in what you feel about the lateness.'

Such a non-punitive response to this behaviour-as-communication can often enable the client to feel safe enough to recognise the possibility of emerging anger behind the lateness.

Medication

For those who are in a position either to recommend or prescribe medication a dilemma often arises. Is the prescription of anxiolytic drugs a useful way of reducing the fear of feelings and offering temporary relief from the unbearable 'stuckness' of complicated grief? Or is it a message to the client about the unacceptability either of the protective depression or of the avoided feelings? This latter message would simply reinforce the dampening effects of the drugs. Inappropriate prescribing to dampen the effects of ordinary grief is, unfortunately, still common.

With clients stuck in depression, feelings of guilt or anger may be quick to appear in the prescriber. Thus some prescribing may be more of a response to the doctor-counsellor's guilt that the patient is not getting better (as if the doctor could actually do the grief work for the patient!) rather than to the patient's real needs. Alternatively it may be a response to anger with the patient for evoking depressing experiences in the doctor-counsellor (as if the patient actually wanted to be depressed!).

Not prescribing, on the other hand, may also evoke guilty responses in the doctor-counsellor for not 'taking away' the uncomfortable experiences (as if the drugs actually took away the grief rather than postponing it!). The prescriber may need to take these 'uncomfortable experiences' to supervision. At other times the 'not-prescribing' may itself be an angry punitive response to someone who has become dependent on drugs and is now in a position of need and guilty despair.

There are difficult dilemmas which arise for any prescriber. For some patients who seem inexorably 'stuck' then anxiolytic drugs may help them to accept the 'stuckness', making day-to-day life more bearable. This may enable other life experiences to work some healing, although perhaps not at a very deep level. However, with many patients in grief prescribing more often sets up cycles of dependency, which confirm the client's inability to tolerate the very feelings being avoided, thus reinforcing the depression itself. As attitudes towards drug-prescribing and drug-taking change, both prescriber and drug-user may have feelings of guilt about the drugs, which can often outweigh the useful effects the drugs may have. None the less, careful prescribing for certain patients, in consultation with a psychotherapist or counsellor, is often extremely effective. Sharing these dilemmas with a sensitive colleague or in supervision is strongly recommended.

Leaving a job

If a counsellor absolutely has to leave a job before a counselling relationship has ended it is, clearly, important to give the client as much notice as possible. Sometimes the counsellor faces the dilemma of whether to bring information about her own departure into the counselling relationship at a time when the client may be grappling with her grief from long ago. Generally speaking the longer the client knows, the more time is available to talk about this new loss with the very person who is going to be lost. Helping the client to face up to and grieve the impending loss is an extremely important part of the work. The sudden death of a counsellor would constitute a leaving of a job. It is most important that another experienced counsellor should inform the client and be available to help him with the complex feelings arising out of a further unplanned loss.

DRAWING TOGETHER THE THREADS

In Table 13.1 we have summarised the protective patterns found in the grievers featured in this chapter. We have also summarised the hidden feelings and the way the counsellor has picked up and used these elements. It may take a long time in complicated grief for the client to be able to use the counselling relationship to unblock his grief. The counsellor may require great patience.

Table 13.1 Summary of protective patterns in complicated grief

Griever	Protective behaviour	Denied feelings	Counsellor's responses
1 Mrs Brown	Idealisation of husband.	Hate and anger.	Recognises incomplete picture and hints at possibility of anger.
2 Frank	Vilification of ex-wife.	Pain, sadness and underlying love.	Recognises incomplete picture, hints at sadness and recognises possibility of loving feelings.
3 Christopher	Angry outburst.	Pain, loneliness, also longing for trust and intimacy.	Affirms reality of loss, recognises angry feelings and hints at hurt, notices possible difficulties with trust in the counselling relationship.
4 Martha	Depression as hopelessness.	Anger, hate and guilt, and all other feelings.	Recognises protective nature of depression and fear of feelings. Hints at grief about Tim and anger with him.
5 Peter	Depression as blankness.	Anger, hate and guilt.	Recognises possibility of feelings behind endless words.
6 Vilna	Suicidal thoughts and wishes.	Despair, underlying anger and guilt.	Recognises protective function of suicidal thoughts, despair and hopelessness. Hints at underlying anger or unconscious hope.

The use of clarification and confrontation without punishment, which we have described in this chapter, is by far the most complex skill we have considered so far. It relies not only on picking up the griever's underlying feelings but also uses the counsellor's awareness of the protective nature of certain kinds of behaviour. The counsellor will, of course, reflect on how much of this particular feeling belongs to her and how much to the griever, and on how and when to respond to the behaviour or the underlying feelings, or both. Assessing how complicated a grief might be and whether or when it might be appropriate to refer a client is considered in the next chapter.

SUMMARY

1 Difficulties with empathy, genuineness and acceptance may relate to the counsellor's own experiences of loss or may be a sign of complicated grief in the client or both.
2 Sensitivity and self-awareness are enormously important when working with complicated grief as a way of understanding and of working with certain feelings which are avoided.
3 The counsellor's task is to recognise the protection and its function without colluding in the denial of the avoided feeling.
4 Various patterns of protection from different feelings need to be approached with slightly different counsellor strategies. These are summarised in Table 13.1 in the text.
5 A counsellor may face particularly delicate dilemmas when working with complicated grief. They will require both skill and patience and should all be considered in supervision.

Section V

PROFESSIONAL IMPLICATIONS

14

ASSESSMENT AND REFERRAL

ASSESSMENT SKILLS

We have placed this skill at the end of the book as it is one of the most complex skills a counsellor uses. Paradoxically, of course, these assessment skills are used in the very first meeting or meetings, yet involve at least all the knowledge and skills we have outlined so far.

At the same time as extending empathy and opening ourselves to a client's story of their loss, counsellors are also trying to assess each client's vulnerability and capacity to grieve. The counsellor will have to try to decide what the client needs and whether this can be offered. The client is, of course, also assessing whether the counsellor is right for them. As the counsellor listens, an assessment has to be made of which external factors might be influencing the client's needs at that moment as well as beginning to pick up clues about the internal factors likely to affect the grieving process. Above all the counsellor will be getting a sense of how the client is experiencing the relationship and whether the client wants to form a counselling relationship or not.

The counsellor uses knowledge about such elements as the relevance of early loss history, for instance, to try to assess the risk of breakdown or unmanageable distress for this client during mourning. In listening to the client's story the counsellor also needs to assess the network of available support, as well as whether the grief work is already under way. In particular, an assessment has to be made based on the relationship and how it is developing, in order to help reach the decision as to whether the skills and experience of the counsellor are appropriate to continue working with this client. There are indeed so many factors affecting the assessment of a client's suitability for loss counselling or psychotherapy that it may be useful to have a checklist such as the one in Table 14.1.

These factors are not simply a list of separate items as described in chapter 4, but rather a set of linked factors which will affect one another. We shall start at one end with the external circumstances affecting the impact of the loss and move towards the more internal factors which also

153

Table 14.1 Factors to be considered in assessing clients' suitability for loss counselling and preferable level of competence in the counsellor

LEVELS \ FACTORS	INCREASING EXPERIENCE AND TRAINING OF COUNSELLOR → INCREASING COMPLEXITY OF RELEVANT FACTORS			
Place of death	at home	in hospital		abroad/isolated
Coincidental losses	one person	two people		more than two
Successive losses	one loss in given period	two losses in quick succession		two or more losses in quicker succession
Nature of loss	expected non-traumatic	sudden non-traumatic		sudden, traumatic or horrendous
Networks	supportive community	less supportive community		person detatched from community
Cultural background	loss-accepting culture	culture ambivalent towards loss		loss-denying culture
Intimacy level of lost relationship	elderly parent or other relative	adult sibling	young sibling	spouse or lover	child
Life-stage of griever	not in transition	some transition (e.g. menopause)	considerable transition (e.g. adolescence)	transition of childhood
Grief history of griever	previous losses largely grieved	most losses grieved		previous losses stirred by current losses
Emotional complexity of relationship lost	straightforward relationship, conflicts largely tolerated	more complex relationship, less tolerance of conflict		complex relationship, guilt and ambivalence largely denied

Table 14.1 (continued)

LEVELS / FACTORS	INCREASING EXPERIENCE AND TRAINING OF COUNSELLOR → INCREASING COMPLEXITY OF RELEVANT FACTORS		
Degree of isolation and capacity to trust others	relates (either well or badly) to more than one person; capacity to trust	relates to at least one other person with some trust	few, if any, relationships; little capacity to trust
Ability to express feelings	able to express feelings and verbalise thoughts	intellectualises many feelings, thoughts get stuck	little feeling expression, muddled thoughts
Ability to tolerate feelings	able to tolerate disturbing thoughts and feelings	some disturbing thoughts and feelings but manages these, largely through use of protective patterns	many disturbing thoughts and feelings, some debilitating use of protective patterns
Desire for change	willingness to face the loss and the changes it brings	reluctance to face the loss and subsequent changes	fear or even terror of facing the loss
Preparedness to trust in counselling relationship	open and essentially trusting of the counselling process	apprehensive about trusting either the person or the process of counselling	extreme difficulty in trusting, or, alternatively, inappropriate over-ready trust

affect the loss. These internal factors, which link with growth of the relationship for the client will, of course, also affect the counselling relationship itself. The effect of the various factors also needs to be understood cumulatively. Thus, while one or two 'more complex' factors may well be manageable by the less experienced counsellor, as the number and degree of more complex factors affecting the client and his loss increases, so the counsellor will need to draw on greater training and experience.

The components of the checklist in Table 14.1 are based on extensive research and experience, but there are few discrete categories in this complex area and the descriptions are somewhat simplified. However, such a checklist can serve as a useful working tool, both to assess someone's suitability for counselling or psychotherapy, as well as for trying to assess the complexity of the loss and grief in any particular individual. The description of a counsellor's competency in terms of 'increasing experience and training' refers to the period of supervised counselling practice, and 'introductory' through to 'substantial' levels of training. (These terms will be clarified in chapter 16.) We know that some inexperienced and minimally trained counsellors can sometimes provide just what is needed for a particular individual even with a range of 'complex factors'. We also know, sometimes only too well, how experienced psychotherapists may struggle with just one or two 'complex factors' when these touch their own areas of vulnerability. The factors down the left-hand side are not to be seen as discrete in themselves but rather as a general guide to what tends to complicate grief. It is, of course, the way in which previous losses or other complicating factors have been understood and worked through, rather than just the factors themselves, which affects the course of grief and also the counselling relationship.

In general, where the client is well supported, the grief work is under way and the counsellor senses a developing relationship, the counsellor will probably decide to continue counselling, supported by the necessary supervision. In this case, other factors will be less likely to block the counselling process. Counselling will recognise the grief work which has already been achieved and will enable the work to continue.

Sometimes, however, the counsellor may sense the client's difficulty in relating and may pick up hints of early and damaging loss history. There may also be recognition that the grief process seems to be blocked, possibly by some ingrained protective pattern. Usually the counsellor, in regular supervision, will be able to use the skills outlined in chapter 13 to help work through the protective pattern and the underlying feelings. Sometimes, however, referral to an experienced psychotherapist, who can work more extensively with the early loss history, may be necessary. If a counsellor is particularly concerned about a client's capacity to grieve without provoking a serious breakdown or mental illness, then a psychiatric assessment from a psychotherapeutically oriented psychiatrist can also be helpful in ascertaining whether counselling or psychotherapy is appropriate for this person at this time.

Of course these factors affect different individuals differently but when more than a few of the factors on the right-hand side of Table 14.1 are present, then this particular client may not be able to use counselling or psychotherapy at all. Further, certain other phenomena and circumstances in a client's life are generally considered to be contraindications for suitability for counselling or psychotherapy. These include: chronic alcoholism or drug addiction; long-term hospitalisation; more than one course of ECT; gross destructive or self-destructive behaviour; and extremely resistant or severe symptoms of fear or obsessive behaviour, where it may be wiser to leave such 'protections' intact. Some people who express their psychic pain through bodily (somatic) pain may also be unsuitable for grief therapy, particularly where the somatic pain is resistant and the client is not receptive to psychological ways of understanding. For such people grief may indeed remain stuck and the best help to be given may be to offer 'support' counselling to help shore up their protective patterns.

REFERRAL SKILLS

In thinking about referral it is important to remember that the client may seek referral rather than the counsellor initiating it. However the initial thoughts arise concerning referral, there are three important considerations: first 'Why refer?', second 'When to refer?' and third 'How to refer?'. The counsellor may find reasons during the initial assessment for immediate referral, or other reasons may arise much later in the relationship. The client may also have good reasons after the first session, or much later in the relationship, to seek referral. Sometimes we refer too early: sometimes too late. Sometimes we are insensitive to the need to refer and sometimes we concur too quickly with a request, or an imagined request for referral. We must constantly monitor our work, both on our own and with our supervisor, to understand the complexity of the problem and the true basis of our decision.

Reasons for immediate referral

Some of the reasons for immediate referral of a client were outlined in the assessment section above, and concerned the degree of fit between experience and training of the counsellor and the factors suggesting complicated grieving in the client. In general the greater the complexity for the client, the greater the need for sensitivity, good training and sufficient experience in the counsellor. If the counsellor assesses straight away that she is not suitably trained nor experienced enough to work with this client then this is a good enough reason for immediate referral.

Another reason for immediate referral would be when a client's loss touches a particularly sensitive aspect of the counsellor's own life. If, for example, a client presented with grief for a lost child and the counsellor had had a similar experience which was unresolved, perhaps because it was such a recent event, then the counsellor might decide to refer at that point.

A counsellor might also refer immediately if there were clear practical difficulties such as transport, locality, finances or mutual availability of time. With such incompatibilities it would be more suitable for the client to see someone else.

On such occasions it may be quite clear in the first session that immediate referral is appropriate. However, in other instances this decision cannot be reached in the first or even second session. There are times when the level of make-believe and denial is such that the counsellor may need some time to sense the possibilities within the relationship and to be able to assess what is happening for the client. Thus, referral to an experienced counsellor or a psychotherapist may also be appropriate after a number of sessions or at even later stages in the counselling relationship.

Reasons for late referral

There are times when the relationship between the counsellor and client meets with great difficulty and it is sometimes tempting for the counsellor to refer. Often a discussion of the situation with the supervisor will enable the difficulty to be resolved within the counselling relationship itself, thus allowing the work to continue.

There are other situations which sometimes arise later in the counselling relationship, when a counsellor certainly should consider referral. For instance, a sudden bereavement for the counsellor, particularly if the loss is similar to that being experienced by the client, might make it necessary to refer. Another example might be when the counsellor realises, through something which suddenly emerges in the counselling relationship, that the client's loss has evoked a large area of unresolved feeling from the counsellor's past. In consultation with a supervisor the counsellor may decide that counselling of clients should stop for a period; perhaps with the counsellor seeking counselling for a while. Alternatively the supervisor may suggest that the counsellor have extra counselling help with her own grief for the very purpose of enabling the established counselling relationship to continue. Wherever possible it is, of course, preferable to continue the counselling relationship once it is under way, and not create yet another loss. There are many reasons for this, but with loss counselling in particular the potential for feelings of rejection and the propensity to feel guilt are very frequent and powerful. In these circumstances referral can exacerbate feelings of rejection and guilt in the client. The supervisor has an important role in helping the counsellor with a decision to refer. This includes both the arrangements for the referral of the client, as well as ensuring that the counsellor gets help.

When referral has to happen, it is essential that the 'referring counsellor' remembers that the client may well feel 'as if it were her fault'. Therefore the reasons for referral should be as clear as possible. The 'receiving' counsellor will need to work through the referral with any referred clients who may well have guilt feelings and, almost certainly, feelings of anger towards the initial counsellor for 'rejecting' them.

Timing of referrals

We have recognised above that it is often very difficult to assess, in the first or even the second session, whether or not referral is appropriate. This is a difficult skill. It may also be difficult to get the timing right and some of the difficulties in referral timing can be understood and worked through in supervision.

Trainee counsellors are sometimes inclined to refer earlier than appropriate, particularly when they fear the strong feelings which often emerge quite quickly in loss counselling sessions. This can result in the counsellor feeling unsure that they can maintain the 'secure-base' for the griever. Supervision often helps to clarify the counsellor's feelings in such a case and usually enables the relationship to continue.

Sometimes counsellors in training, and indeed other more experienced counsellors, have the enthusiastic, but somewhat omnipotent idea, that they ought to be able to do anything and everything. They cannot then distinguish between recognition of their own limitations, on the one hand, and 'failure' in the work, on the other. They may then fail to refer appropriately early. Supervision can help trainees to see when recognising their own limitations is an important part of professional development and is not a failure in the relationship.

Less often, perhaps, a counsellor can become so overinvolved with the bereaved person that they do not make an appropriate referral soon enough. This may arise through a fear of separation, which the counsellor picks up from the griever, but does not recognise or respond to appropriately. Supervision can enable the counsellor to recognise the client's fear of separation and can help the counsellor to work with this. If a referral is indeed appropriate at this stage, the supervisor may need to help the counsellor with her fear of failure in the relationship. This fear may have contributed to the counsellor's failure to understand the client's needs in the first place.

There are times when an early referral or a late referral is appropriate. Good referrals require considerable counselling skill. Using supervision to explore the counsellor's own thoughts and feelings is important in attempting to clarify the reasons, timing and responsibility for referral.

Method of referral

As mentioned immediately above, good referrals require considerable counselling skills. It is important to be as clear and unambiguous as possible, and to attempt to state your feelings and responsibility as straight-forwardly as possible to prevent the client sometimes feeling 'as if it were her fault'. It is important to clarify your role and responsibility in the referral process and to recognise the client's feeling in response to your referral suggestion. Here are two attempts to be open and clear with Joe as it becomes obvious early in the relationship that it is appropriate to refer him to someone more experienced.

Early stage referral: Joe

You will remember Joe from Exercises 9.1, 9.3, 9.4, and from chapter 13. It is now his third session and you feel distinctly puzzled at his odd behaviour. He seems lifeless and listless. You feel increasingly uncomfortable about his capacity to relate to you and his difficulty with expressing feelings. You decide to try and share this with him. You might say either of the following:

'Joe, I'm feeling a bit uncomfortable about what's happening in here right now. I'm not sure I'm going to be able to help you much at this stage. I think I might like to get another opinion on this... How does this idea strike you?'
OR
'Joe, I think I'm sensing some feelings in you that may be difficult for you and I think they are difficult for me too at this point. I'm wondering if perhaps you and I might get some help with that?'

If Joe was able to hear that the counsellor was neither accusing him nor punishing him, he might recognise that she was not the right person to work with him on those difficulties at that time. The counsellor needs to recognise and understand any feelings of rejection evoked in Joe. This would help Joe to recognise and work with such feelings with either the referring or the 'receiving' counsellor to whom the referral is made.

Referral at an early stage may be relatively straightforward if there has been very little time for a relationship to develop and there are thus likely to be less strong feelings of rejection in the client. When, however, there are reasons to refer later in the relationship, then the feelings aroused in the client by the referral are likely to be much stronger, and to need more time to be worked through. Let us think about the feelings which might be evoked in Alice, whom you will also remember from Exercises 9.1 and 9.3, when her counsellor decides to refer her for more specialised help. You will remember the complex difficulties she faced in grieving Brendan's death.

This was exacerbated by her husband's refusal to accept Brendan's addiction and also by the general persecution of Aids sufferers in the community. First let us consider the referral itself.

Late stage referral: Alice

Let us imagine you have been working with Alice now for over a year. She has gradually begun to trust you and has survived the painful anniversary of Brendan's death, but somehow things don't seem to be moving. Alice has suddenly become icily cold and seems to be withdrawing from you and the counselling relationship. This withdrawal is puzzling. You discuss this with your supervisor and together you both realise that Alice may need help from someone with more skills and experience than you. You might say either of the following:

'Alice, I'd like to take a look at where we are. I recognise that we've done a lot of work together but I'm thinking that perhaps there may be some work you need to do with someone who's more experienced than me. I wonder what you think about this?'
OR
'Alice, we've worked together for a year now and I've seen your courage in facing and grieving Brendan's death. Now I'm beginning to wonder whether perhaps facing Brendan's death has brought you into contact with even deeper losses in your life. Perhaps you and I could talk about whether I'm the right person to continue working with you from now on in considering these deeper losses?'

It is always difficult to predict how grievers will respond to a counsellor's thoughts and recommendations about referral. Some people feel relief at the counsellor's recognition of their difficulties without judging or blaming them, and relief that they themselves do not need to ask for more trained help. They might also feel sadness at the thought of losing the current counselling relationship. This in its turn may touch off other sadnesses from past separations, which will need to be recognised and 'contained' in some way so that they can be 'carried over' to the next relationship. You might then say something like the following in response to someone's sadness.

Counsellor: I'm feeling sad too about our separation ... and I wonder if the sadness in here is touching the pain of the great sadness out there about your mother who you lost long ago?
Client: Mm – yes, I suppose so.
Counsellor: I guess one of our tasks is to somehow parcel up that sadness about your mother for now, so that you can

then carry it on to your work with your new counsellor. The sadness we share in here now about our separation is different from the sadness about earlier times, which you need to carry alone again.

Returning now to Alice, she seemed to accept the need for referral to someone more experienced yet her response was full of anger. You were as clear as you could be about your responsibility in referring, yet for Alice the very notion of 'passing-her-on', however rational she knew it to be, had awakened raw experiences of rejection from earlier times. Her natural response to rejection was one of anger.

Alice: (Angrily) Right! You may as well ring 'the bin' straight away!

Counsellor: Alice, I hear your anger towards me and I guess that in some way it must *feel* as if I'm rejecting you just like you were rejected in the past.

Alice: (Resentfully) Well, you are rejecting me aren't you – you're sending me away aren't you?

Counsellor: (Firmly and gently) No, Alice. I'm not *sending* you away I'm suggesting you seek someone better able to work with you on the losses from long ago. A part of you knows that's right and that this now is different from being sent away. Another part of you is, I guess, remembering very painful feelings associated with being sent away so that it feels *as if* I were sending you away. The very painful feelings of rejection you are experiencing in here are probably making you feel angry with me now?

Alice: Yes, I am feeling angry, I know I shouldn't be.

Counsellor: Your angry feelings in here certainly make sense to *me* as a response to the rejection which you remember so acutely from then.

As Alice was gradually able to recognise, express and have her angry feelings accepted, she was able to understand that the real rejection happened in the past. Sadly she now needed to change her therapist to continue with the work. As so often happens, when her anger was understood it began to subside and she was able to see that the counsellor was not actively rejecting her. She could then begin to experience her sadness at the separation from this counsellor. Recognition, expression and acceptance of the feelings evoked by the referral are necessary for a successful referral to take place. This very referral process may enable the griever to begin to separate the real rejection, which happened in the past but is remembered in the present, from the necessary but, of course, painful separation from the current counsellor. The way the 'receiving' therapist works with the feelings of grief associated with the separation from the original counsellor will be an important factor in creating trust in the new relationship. Professional jealousies have no place here!

A client may occasionally seek referral as a way of avoiding painful issues, but generally a client who is avoiding difficult feelings with a counsellor will simply miss sessions or prevent issues being discussed in the session. If the relationship is well established the client is likely to hope, however secretly, that the counsellor will notice and help with the difficulties. The request for referral in this case can be seen as a metaphor for the need to avoid pain or to avoid relationships (see chapters 10 and 13).

As mentioned earlier, clients also seek referral for appropriate reasons. When referral is suggested by a client then the counsellor needs to remember that it is a measure of the trust in the relationship that the client has been able to come and discuss the referral. It would be all too easy to just stay away or try to approach someone else without the counsellor's knowledge, or perhaps do both. In this case it is the counsellor who needs to remember that this referral is different from the counsellor's experiences of hurtful rejections from the past! The counsellor may also need to hold on to the recognition of the trust, which has brought the client with this request. The counsellor may use supervision to help work out which kind of 'referral' is being sought.

Assessment and referral are complex skills. They rely on the fundamental attitudes and basic skills mentioned earlier, on practical training and on continuous supervision of the counselling relationship. The next chapter deals with the function and processes of supervision.

SUMMARY

1 Assessing the suitability of a client for counselling; requires a very complex set of skills.
2 The sense of relationship, the internal factors and, to a lesser extent, the external factors all need to be taken into consideration in assessing a client's need.
3 Reasons for immediate referral include non-suitability of client and counsellor; recent counsellor losses; practical difficulties.
4 Reasons for later referrals include the counsellor having a sudden loss; lack of counsellor training and experience so unable to work with 'difficult' client material emerging later in the counselling relationship. Supervision, however, will often enable these difficulties to be worked through and the referral to be avoided.
5 Reasons for inappropriate timing of referrals include fear of strong feelings; overinvolvement with a client; omnipotent feelings; poor assessment skills.

6 In making referrals it is important for the counsellor to be clear and openly accepting of responsibility for the referral. Client feelings of guilt, anger or rejection need to be recognised, accepted and worked through.

15

SUPERVISION

FUNCTIONS OF SUPERVISION

Supervision has been referred to in several chapters in this book. We now come to discuss what we really mean, and why we consider it to be so important. The word 'supervision' in counselling refers to a relationship between a counsellor and another, usually more experienced counsellor, who ideally has some further training in counselling supervision. It is sometimes called 'consultative support' in order to avoid confusion with other meanings of 'supervisor', which entail ideas of 'inspector' or 'overseer', with the corresponding suggestions of incompetence or formal assessment. Practising counsellors meet regularly, either individually or in small groups (three to four people), with their supervisors or with peer groups to talk through and reflect upon their counselling sessions. The choice of individual, small group or peer group supervision might be simply pragmatic, and based on availability. However, it is important to recognise that peer group supervision is only suitable for experienced counsellors, and even then it should not be the only supervision. A fairly typical duration and frequency for individual supervision would be 1 hour every fortnight, and for peer and small group supervision 1½ hours every fortnight.

In chapters 9, 10 and 13 we have tried to give some idea of how counselling attitudes, sensitivity and knowledge might look when translated into 'skills'. We also likened the integration of counselling skills into the counselling relationship to the integration of skills required in the co-ordination necessary to ride a bicycle. But of course the counselling relationship is more than that; it is a living interchange between two human beings, who are both experiencing and learning within that relationship. One of the ways in which the counsellor learns from, and about, the counselling relationship and about how to develop it more effectively, is through this confidential supervision relationship. In supervision a counsellor is able to focus on the interaction with the client in a collaborative and supportive environment. The supervisor recognises and works with the feelings experienced in the counselling session, as well as those experienced in the supervisory session.

Such a 'place for feelings' is very necessary, for in choosing to enter the world of other people's losses counsellors are entering something different from the normal and the everyday. There are times when it may seem barely worth while to the counsellor. Clients can be consistently ungrateful, can get stuck in suicidal feelings and do, albeit occasionally, succeed in committing suicide. Counsellors can think they have lost their way and feel useless, helpless and drained. It would hardly be surprising, then, that counsellors can come to believe they have nothing more to give, or have been a failure. At times like this it is tempting to 'soldier on', to 'keep the head down', to 'get on with it' and not make time to reflect in supervision on what is going on in the counselling relationship. Individuals, teams and organisations can all collude in this process of 'head down', 'soldier on' and denial of the necessity for supervision. This denial may occur out of the mistaken, but common, belief that remembering and reflecting on pain 'only makes it worse'. Yet it is this very reflecting and sharing, in the context of a secure and professional supervisory relationship, which can offer comfort and care for the counsellor's struggle with the client. Supervision can also offer a place to reflect upon the skills and interventions which are being used, as well as those which are being avoided. It can then enable the counsellor to ponder the reasons for avoidance of certain skills or feelings; or to wonder why certain rules of counselling practice are suddenly particularly difficult to follow.

A loss counsellor then can expect supervision to function in three ways.

1   As a safe and secure base in which to feel, and to reflect upon feelings, images and associations which arise. This is sometimes called the restorative function.
2   As a place to develop appropriate skills and abilities through reflecting upon and learning from the nitty-gritty of the relationship. This is sometimes called the formative function.
3   As a place to reflect as honestly and openly as possible about the quality of the counselling work and its relationship to professional standards and codes of practice. This is sometimes called the normative function.

These 'restorative, formative and normative functions of supervision' (Proctor, 1988), although theoretically possible to describe as if they were discrete entities, are in practice seldom totally separate. We shall start by describing each function in turn and then give a brief illustration of how they interweave.

The restorative function

For an inexperienced counsellor a sense of security will be enhanced through training. This fosters self-awareness and acceptance, and confirms and develops skills. None the less, even for the most experienced counsellor the very strong feelings associated with the void, emptiness, suicidal despair and essential loneliness of human existence, can emerge in the process of grieving and evoke fear and insecurity. The counsellor who wishes to remain receptive to this experience in others, needs to be allowed to feel such emotional disturbance within the safer setting of the supervisory relationship. To create a safe environment for this type of exploration the supervisor needs to demonstrate the attitudes of empathy, warmth and genuineness, and hence create an accepting environment. In such a climate the counsellor can feel secure enough to explore, ponder and reflect upon the counsellor–client relationship in a way which ensures and develops the effectiveness of that relationship. We can draw a parallel here between supervision and John Bowlby's work on attachment.

In chapter 1 we mentioned Bowlby's work, in which he showed that parents who are secure within themselves, and who are not overanxious about themselves or their world, offer their children a secure base from which to explore. This, in turn, leads to the children feeling secure enough to be able to explore, enjoy and understand the world. Of course, children will get hurt and frightened in the course of their explorations, but they will return to the secure base for comfort and healing before setting out again. In a similar way the supervisor, who is personally secure, offers a 'secure base' where the counsellor can return for comfort and healing. The counsellor is then in a better position to 'set out' and offer a secure and predictable relationship to a client. This will be very necessary for a client who is hurt, frightened and in need of security in a world which has become chaotic and unpredictable through loss.

To offer such a secure base the supervisors too need their own supervision. A further way in which the security of supervision is enhanced is through a clear contract. This needs to be negotiated along the lines of the 'Code of Practice' section of the British Association for Counselling's (BAC) Code of Ethics and Practice for the Supervision of Counsellors.

Obviously the restorative function of supervision has similarities to personal counselling, but only in as far as the environment of acceptance is essential to create trust. Beyond that the focus is different. In supervision the primary focus is the counsellor's client; in personal counselling the focus would be on the counsellor.

The formative function

For an inexperienced counsellor supervision often focuses on the task of relating theoretical ideas, such as those outlined in chapters 1 to 8, to the actual practice of counselling. There is likely therefore to be a substantial training aspect to supervision in the early stages. The counsellor will also be helped to look very closely at which skills were used in the session and which were not. Further areas of exploration would be to look at the consequences of these interventions, and to help the counsellor become more aware of responses, and sometimes reactions, to the client and in return to consider the client's reactions. As the counsellor gains experience, supervision focuses more and more on understanding what is going on in the relationship. We sometimes use the word 'process' to mean 'what-is-going-on-in-the-relationship'. Reflecting upon this process of the counselling relationship and trying to understand the particular pattern of grief constitutes the 'meat', as it were, of supervision. Other less conscious processes relating to supervison will be considered later in this chapter.

The normative function

Supervisors within almost any context will have some responsibility to ensure that the counsellor's work is appropriate and falls within defined ethical standards. Given that the primary purpose of supervision is to ensure that the counsellor is addressing the needs of the client, the supervisor will be concerned with ethical issues of counselling. This includes concern about confidentiality, respect for the client's beliefs and values, and maintenance of the boundaries between counselling and friendship. The supervisor also needs to recognise whether the counsellor is too depleted by the work to continue counselling; or too affected by the losses brought to the work to continue without having either a break from counselling, further training, personal counselling or even all three. The supervisor's task within this function is to monitor the overall quality of the work. The BAC publishes Codes of Ethics and Practice for Counsellors and for those using Counselling Skills, in addition to the Code for Supervisors mentioned earlier.

The interweaving of supervisory functions

To show how these various supervisory functions interweave in the supervision of loss counselling we shall return to Angie's story (chapter 10).

Angie's story

You will remember that Angie was able to pick up the threads of her life again after Oliver's death: not without great pain and sorrow, but with increased sensitivity and a new maturity. After that there followed a period of enormous personal and professional development for Angie. Gradually she was able to invest her renewed energy into her work and grow in confidence and personal strength. About 3½ years after Oliver's death Angie met Paul, who himself was suffering loss. His ex-wife Sally, from whom he had separated four years previously, but who had continued to live down the road, had decided to move to northern Scotland taking his 4-year-old daughter

Katie. Angie not only 'knew' about loss in the historical sense of having experienced loss herself, she also 'knew' about loss in the sense of knowing that the feelings of grief need to be heard and understood. She knew that it would take time for ambivalent feelings to be disentangled and resolved and that the process cannot be rushed. Therefore she was not only able to wait for Paul to grieve the profound loss of Sally and Katie, but was also able to help him in his grief. Knowing that Paul's loving feelings towards Sally and Katie did not prevent loving feelings growing in their own relationship, Angie was able to tell Paul a great deal about Oliver. This allowed Angie to treasure the precious memories of the man who had died so young. Angie and Paul's relationship developed through their separate griefs; they were married two years later and went on to have two children of their own.

Over the years, as the children became more independent, Angie realised that she was interested in going forward for selection as a bereavement counsellor. In thinking about the selection process, she wondered whether the wound of Oliver's death 10 years earlier had healed enough for her to be in a position to offer herself for counselling training. She thought that it had.

Angie was indeed selected as a counsellor, took part in initial training and began working with her first clients. She had group supervision at the training centre and saw her individual supervisor once a fortnight.

One day a new client, Debbie, came in to see Angie and quickly burst into tears. The following is the story she had to tell.

Debbie's story

Debbie was a student and had recently gone to university. The day before she had left home for university she had received a letter out of the blue from her boyfriend, John, her first love, saying quite coldly that the relationship was finished. He was going to college, she to university, and their ways ought to part. Debbie had been distraught at this news and had sought comfort from her mother, but her mother seemed to reject her feelings and kept insisting that 'there were other fish in the sea'. This made Debbie feel even worse and it was at that point that she had sought counselling at the agency where Angie worked.

Two days after this initial session Angie was able to take the work to her supervisor, David. In Exercise 15.1 on the following page we give an account of this supervision session. We also give you a chance to look for examples of the restorative, formative and normative functions of supervision.

Exercise 15.1 A typical supervision session

The first memory Angie had was that Debbie had been very distressed, and that she was grieving the loss of her young man, John, at much the same age she had been when Oliver died. She then remembered that she had wondered momentarily whether she should refer Debbie to someone else. However, she had felt secure enough in herself to leave the idea of referral and get on with the work with Debbie in the session. In supervision she wanted to review this decision, and to consider further whether the empathic skills she had used had been appropriate and effective. As Angie talked with her supervisor, David, about her initial assessment she realised that she had noticed three crucial factors which had suggested to her the appropriateness of a counselling relationship for Debbie. First Debbie had talked of student friends in a way that made Angie think she was well supported. Second Angie noticed Debbie's open distress and anger, which seemed to indicate that the grief work was under way. Finally Angie had sensed a growing trust and developing relationship as the counselling session progressed. Angie herself felt well supported in the supervisory relationship so she realised, encouraged by her supervisor, that she should continue with Debbie rather than refer.

As the supervision session proceeded Angie remembered Debbie's anger, and also began to remember, with poignant intensity, how angry she herself had felt when she had experienced feelings of abandonment by Oliver. Gradually as she talked about those feelings of loss, abandonment and anger, she became aware that Debbie's anger was different from her own. However, she realised that she had the capacity to understand and empathise with Debbie. She realised, with David's help, that she had grieved Oliver enough to be able to work with Debbie on Debbie's grief. This enabled her to focus on the feelings in relation to Debbie which she was still aware of from the session. She could remember the interventions she had used, and reflect on what their effect might have been on the counselling relationship. She could then consider alternative interventions and think with her supervisor about how she might have ended the session more effectively. This led on to a brief discussion about the particular importance of firm boundaries in loss counselling.

Use the space below to identify examples of the restorative, formative and normative functions of supervision.

In the supervision session outlined in Exercise 15.1 we have shown how the three main functions of supervision interweave. At the beginning of the session, supervision is mainly formative, as Angie reflects on the relationship with Debbie. In reflecting on her feelings of anger the function of the supervision moves into the restorative mode; and then back into the formative mode, as Angie returns the focus to understanding Debbie and working with Debbie's anger. There are further examples of the movement from formative to reflective and back again before the final part of the supervision, which is normative.

USES OF FEELINGS

The counsellor's feelings

In the above description of a supervisory session we have focused on the various feelings which are evoked in the counsellor and which are a particularly important part of supervision. First of all this focusing helps the counsellor to discover whether these feelings belong more to the client or more to the counsellor. If they belong to the counsellor it is important to establish whether they can be contained within the supervisory session, and then used to understand more about the client; or whether they signal the need for personal counselling for the counsellor. This focus on the counsellor's feelings is both restorative, in that it helps contain the feelings naturally evoked by working with loss, and formative in that the discovery may be made that certain feelings, experienced by the sensitive counsellor, may well be the very feelings denied by the client. Awareness of the existence and nature of all these feelings is an important part of the counsellor's development.

We shall now return to Angie to look in more detail at how the supervisor helps the counsellor use her feelings remembered from the counselling session. In her supervision session with David we see how Angie's feelings were contained and then used to give a clue to Debbie's difficulties.

Use of counsellor's feelings to locate denied feelings in the client

In the session described in Exercise 15.1 Angie found that her feelings about Oliver, reawakened by the counselling work, could be heard and contained within the supervision session. She was then able to focus back on to her session with Debbie. As she did this she became aware of an intensely sad and aching feeling in herself, which she had first felt as she listened to Debbie raging about this 'awful' John. Debbie seemed still to be protecting herself from feelings of pain and sadness by raging at and vilifying John. (This is similar to Frank's behaviour in chapter 13.) Angie seemed to sense the feelings, which Debbie dared not. David, her supervisor, in pondering about these feelings with her, helped her to see that not only the anger but also the feelings of sadness and pain belonged to Debbie. They then discussed ways in which Angie might reflect back the anger and rage which Debbie was expressing, and hint at the sadness and longing of which Debbie seemed unaware (see chapter 13). This would give Debbie an opportunity, within the context of the counselling relationship, to experience the feelings of which she was afraid.

Use of counsellor's feelings to recognise the counsellor's need

When the feelings stirred up in a counsellor by a particular client keep distracting the counsellor from the counselling relationship, they may be signalling to the counsellor that certain ungrieved losses in her own life need attention. The following account is given by a counsellor who experienced powerful feelings in the counselling session, which later in supervision she recognised as her own.

'About 10 years ago now I remember how, towards the end of a counselling session with Jenny, I felt my throat tighten and tears coming to my eyes. Jenny was grieving the loss, through abortion, of the only child she might have had with the man who had just left her.

Of course I might well have shed tears for Jenny in her hitherto unrecognised grief, but my tears here were strangely distracting and I felt uncomfortable and angry in the session. A few days later in my supervision session I was able, in a safe place, to ponder these feelings and discovered great pain and sadness about a miscarriage I had had some 16 years previously. The relationship with the baby's father had also been lost. It became clear that personal material related not just to the miscarriage, but to the relationship itself, had been re-stimulated in me by Jenny's experiences. The exploration of Jenny's experiences had uncovered more grief in me than could be appropriately dealt with in supervision. I felt considerable relief when my supervisor suggested that I should do some further counselling work in order to explore and work through the feelings from my own grief.

On realising that these distractions came from a past experience of mine, I understood what had interfered with my listening to Jenny. After the supervision session I was able to get help with my own grief. When I met Jenny again the following week I was able "to be" with her more fully, undistracted by feelings which belonged to my past.'

This example illustrates how the supervisor had helped this counsellor to express and understand some of her feelings about her own miscarriage, and lost relationship. The counsellor quickly recognised her own need to get help with her grief. This then enabled the counsellor to empathise with Jenny's conscious feelings, as well as focusing on her feelings at the edge of awareness. She was now responding to Jenny the person, rather than simply reacting to material which Jenny had brought.

Not all feelings felt in a session are necessarily distracting. In supervision we will recall many feelings as we remember a session. One example might be that we felt deskilled. Supervision could help us understand whether the deskilled feeling related quite straightforwardly to poor use of skills; or whether feelings of deep insecurity or hopelessness in the client were being experienced by the counsellor, as if they were her own. Obviously many other feelings felt by the counsellor, when recalling a counselling session in supervision, can be used in this way to understand what is happening in the relationship.

In the previous example with Jenny, a source of learning for the counsellor occurred when feelings, expressed by the griever during the session, immediately re-evoked forgotten and unresolved feelings that had gone underground in the counsellor long ago. In supervision she was quickly aware of the feelings and their source and acknowledged what needed to be done. It sometimes happens, however, that feelings or processes from the client do not reach the counsellor's conscious awareness and so she brings them or 'reflects' them unconsciously into the supervision relationship.

Reflected feelings in the parallel process

This phenomenon of unconscious material from the counselling relationship finding its way into the supervisory relationship was first pointed out by Harold Searles (1955). He described how the processes in the one relationship are repeated or reflected in the processes in the other relationship. This is the basis for what is called the parallel process which happens frequently in supervision.

When the counsellor unconsciously parallels the client's behaviour in supervision it can throw light on the counselling relationship. This happened to one of us recently in supervision when recalling counselling Christopher whom you met in Exercise 9.3 and in chapter 13.

'Christopher talked of his lover Jake who had recently died of Aids. He was angry, isolated and very frightened of trusting me. He came into the first session more or less shouting, "Just how do you think you can help me? Do you know what it feels like to have your lover die? You can't give him back to me can you?" I had responded with something like, "Christopher, you are really angry. Your anger certainly makes sense when you have been so let down. I guess you might be really wary about trusting me in case I let you down too?" I felt reasonably sure that this response was appropriate yet Christopher replied with a "Yes, but why should I trust you anyway?" And

173

so the session continued with Christopher apparently unable to hear, to take in or to use anything I said. By the end of the session I felt pretty useless.

I took this case to supervision hoping, or so I thought, to get some help with this "difficult" client, but found myself exceedingly resistant to what I usually regarded as excellent supervision. My responses of "Yes, but..." soon reached my supervisor's awareness and she was able to point out how the process of "yes-but-resistance" from the counselling session was being reflected in supervision. Once I had become aware of how I was resisting in supervision I realised that this process of resistance was unnecessary there. I could then reflect with my supervisor on how I might work with, and constructively use, Christopher's process of resistance, rather than just be dragged down and made impotent by it.'

Use of the supervisor's feelings

There is another way in which unconscious material from the counselling session finds its way into the supervisory session. A supervisor may pick up an unconscious feeling, which can arise quite suddenly. In paying attention to this 'stray' feeling the supervisor can often provide reflective illumination for the counsellor. Angie's supervisor, David, picked up just such a strong feeling during the first supervision session soon after Angie had seen her new client Debbie.

You will remember how Debbie had sought comfort from her mother who had ignored Debbie's feelings, insisting that 'There were other fish in the sea'. It was at this point that Debbie had sought counselling. Angie subsequently told David about her session with Debbie. In the following passage David describes part of this supervisory session with Angie.

'I was listening to Angie talking about Debbie's sudden loss and something to do with Debbie's mother, when I noticed Angie's curious blankness. Then I found that I wasn't really listening to Angie any more and was feeling inexplicably angry. I quickly reflected on whether I might be feeling angry about anything in my own life outside the session. I thought not. I returned to Angie, pretty certain that this feeling in me was something to do with Angie and possibly also with her relationship with Debbie. I stopped Angie's talk with some difficulty and invited her to reflect on whether this inexplicable angry feeling which I was experiencing could have anything to do with the counselling relationship between her and Debbie. Angie reflected on this. She gradually became aware that she too had been unable to concentrate fully on Debbie, when Debbie was talking about her mother.

As Angie reflected on her own blankness about Debbie and her mother she found herself beginning to feel angry. At this point I had wondered if this was Debbie's anger, which Angie was beginning to feel (see page 170), but she seemed to draw away from Debbie and towards her own past. She then suddenly remembered telling her own mother of Oliver's diagnosis. Her mother, no doubt trying to be helpful at the time, and perhaps not realising the depth of the relationship between Angie and Oliver, had said something like "Never mind dear, there are other pebbles on the beach". Angie also remembered that she had been so shocked and numbed by the news of Oliver at that point, that she had felt relatively little about her mother's response.

She had subsequently been enabled through counselling (see chapter 10) to express her feelings of grief about Oliver's death and now, in supervision, reflected briefly upon that experience. Her sense was that the "wound" had largely healed. It was then that she began to experience and to express anger about her own mother's response. This was anger which she had not been able to feel at the time of Oliver's death and which had gone underground. Having been unable to experience or express her own anger with her own mother then, Angie had been unable later to recognise that Debbie was angry with *her* mother now.

I then understood why Angie had been unable to experience the angry feelings in the session with Debbie. I also understood why she had needed to bring them unconsciously, masked by her blankness, into the supervision session. Once Angie had expressed anger about her own mother's similar remarks, she found that she was still angry. This at last was Debbie's anger which had been denied in the counselling session. We were then able to focus on the related counselling tasks. She could then see that Debbie might be needing to recognise, understand and accept her anger with her mother, rather than just her anger with John for leaving her.'

These examples show two ways in which unconscious material appears in the supervision session. Others occur whenever processes which happen in the counselling session are, often without the counsellor's awareness, reflected or 'paralleled' in supervision. The supervisor's awareness of these processes is an enormously useful contribution to the understanding of the counselling relationship.

In this chapter we have considered the three main functions of supervision and tried to show how these interrelate in practice. We have also tried to show how both the counsellor's and the supervisor's feelings constitute a rich and necessary resource for understanding the counselling process. What has been implied throughout this chapter, but perhaps needs stating more explicitly, is that it is the quality of the relationship between the counsellor and the supervisor which is paramount. It is when both counsellor and supervisor can drop their judgemental attitudes, face the anxieties inherent for both in the supervisory relationship and manage to be genuine with each other, that the supervision is likely to be most effective.

We have talked here of the necessity of supervision for all counsellors, and of the special quality of supervision for all those working with loss and grief. The importance of supervision is highlighted by BAC in its scheme for the accreditation of counsellors. Counsellors are required to show a commitment to ongoing supervision and continued personal development through training.

Supervision itself has training-like qualities in its formative function, but cannot replace a training course in counselling skills or counselling. Any more advanced training course in counselling will include either group or individual supervision as part of the course. In the next chapter we shall outline the basic issues in counselling training.

SUMMARY

1 Supervision is a relationship between either one or several loss counsellors and a more experienced counsellor (working as a supervisor). It focuses on the well-being of the clients and the care and development of the counsellors.

2 Care for the counsellor is particularly important in the lonely business of loss counselling, where the pain of grief is a consistent element of the work.

3 The tendency in our culture to deny pain can lead to a similar tendency to deny the need for supervision.

4 Supervision functions in three main ways:
   a) As a restorative base where the feelings stirred up by grief work may be expressed, contained and reflected upon.
   b) As a formative or developmental forum for studying the theoretical implications, the interventions and the processes of the counselling relationship.
   c) As a place for monitoring the quality of counselling through such normative elements as maintaining appropriate boundaries and adhering to Codes of Ethics and Practice.

5 Supervisory activities sometimes fulfil more than one function simultaneously, and at other times supervision moves almost imperceptibly from one function to another.

6 Some feelings and processes which are not conscious in the counselling

relationship may be brought unconsciously into the supervisory relationship. The supervisor's awareness and use of this material is an integral part of supervision.

16

TRAINING IN LOSS
COUNSELLING SKILLS

A major aim of this book so far has been to use the reader's own experience as an integral part of learning about loss counselling. We have invited you, wherever possible, to see how your experiences relate to ideas about loss counselling.

In Exercises 1.1, 1.2 and 1.3 we asked you to draw on your knowledge and personal experience of how children and parents feel when they are separated from one another. In Exercise 2.1 we invited you to remember the helpful, or indeed not-so-helpful, responses which you received at a time of loss or other difficulty, and then to reflect upon whether these linked with the counsellor attitudes which studies have shown to be effective. In Exercise 8.3 we suggested you recall the feelings associated with losses in your own life, to share these feelings, wherever possible, with a friend or colleague and then to compare your own feelings with those from research studies on loss. We have also invited you, at various times, to identify with some of our own experiences, as a way of illustrating, more personally, the ideas we were trying to outline.

A mere 'book relationship', however, provides only very limited scope for drawing on the experience of either writer or reader. On a training course about loss counselling it is different. There the experiences of learners (or trainees) can be expressed and shared with other course members. In addition a skilled counselling trainer will be able to listen empathically, to demonstrate the therapeutic attitudes and to draw out new learning from individual and group experiences. This kind of learning through experiencing, usually called experiential learning, is an integral part of all counselling training and of learning how to work with the grieving. In this final chapter we shall outline very briefly the basic components of counselling training in general and how these might relate to loss counselling training in particular. We then offer some guidelines for consideration when selecting a course, followed by a brief word to loss counselling course trainers, before finishing with our thoughts about endings.

BASIC COMPONENTS OF A LOSS COUNSELLING COURSE

It follows from the above that a knowledge of our own loss history and a re-experiencing of our own griefs are important aspects of the developing self-awareness associated with training in loss counselling. The use of counselling skills outlined in chapters 9 and 10 is another basic component. The use of such skills with peer learners on a course enables them in turn to experience more of their own losses. These, together with acquiring knowledge about loss and about the counselling model being used, constitute the basic components of counselling training. Although we will discuss these three components of self-awareness, skills and knowledge separately they are, of course, interwoven on a counselling course. Thus the skills of one trainee will be facilitating the experiential learning of another, the varied experiences of a number of different people will enhance the knowledge of the group, and further external knowledge will add to personal development. The interrelatedness of these three elements, important in all aspects of counselling training, is particularly obvious in the supervised counselling practice. One of the main aims of supervision on a training course is to help trainees to integrate these three elements into their counselling practice.

Self-awareness

The experiential nature of loss counselling training may initially be challenging for those unused to this style of learning. Yet it is this very learning to develop self-awareness which is most necessary for counsellors. One of the most daunting issues for counselling trainees and trainers alike is that as the training proceeds it inevitably brings disturbance and pain as part of personal change. If it does not, it is unlikely to be effective in developing real self-awareness. The training may be too stressful for some people, particularly those who are still grieving a recent loss. For this reason it is unwise to consider counselling training, let alone loss counselling training, until at least two years after a major loss. The course literature should make this clear.

Counselling training therefore involves a high degree of experiential learning and self-exploration. It is now generally accepted that for all kinds of counselling and psychotherapy 'an unaware counsellor leading an unexamined life is likely to be a liability rather than an asset' (Thorne and Dryden, 1991). Nowhere is this more true than in loss counselling.

Training courses usually offer a self-exploration or personal development group over and above the experiential learning on the course, but given the nature of the learning involved, trainees may also wish to have access to counselling for themselves. This could come from within the institution offering the course or from recognised local resources outside the course itself. People often find that the experience of being counselled is of enormous advantage when starting both counselling training and practising counselling. Some courses insist upon it as a particularly important part of experiential learning. Many of those who reflect back on their counselling training see the self-development aspect as the most valuable for themselves and as the most useful for their work.

Knowledge and counselling models

Knowledge about human loss may be drawn from the fields of psychology, psychoanalysis, sociology, anthropology and theology (see chapters 1, 4, 5, 6, 7 and 12). These can be followed up in the Further Reading section (Appendix B). Different loss counselling training courses will draw on different disciplines and sources of knowledge. The sources of learning about other people's experiences of human loss are legion; films, novels, drama, poetry, opera, TV soaps and drama documentaries, to name but a few.

Psychology and psychoanalysis have offered us a number of models of how humans function in themselves and how they respond to the world around them. Thus, even though there is more consensus nowadays about the core content of counselling courses, these varied models form the intellectual bases of courses. The loss counselling work presented in this book draws from both the person-centred approach within the humanistic tradition and from the 'British school' of psychodynamic psychotherapy. On a counselling training course, the methods used should be consistent with the basic assumptions about human beings which underlie the particular model. So, for instance, a person-centred course would focus, in its methods, on helping trainees to accept and empathise with other trainees' feelings about their losses without judgement or condemnation. The trainees would be helped to become more sensitive to other trainees' feelings and to tolerate with compassion any anxiety awakened in themselves by such strong feelings or by other people's opinions. They would pay particular attention to any possible abuse of power relationships inherent within the training course, as well as within the work with clients. A psychodynamically oriented loss counselling course, while also encouraging such compassion and sensitivity, might lay greater weight on understanding and working with the ways in which we protect ourselves from feelings which are too frightening or too painful to allow into our conscious awareness. They are also likely to focus, for instance, on the way in which feelings of loss experienced at the end of the counselling session may be reflecting feelings about losses experienced in the past.

Skills

The word skills is used to denote the way a counsellor actually behaves in order to affect a particular client outcome. In presenting skills in this book we have drawn on the work of Truax and Carkhuff (1967), in which they studied the relationship between behaviour and outcome. There are many different and largely arbitrary ways of breaking down or combining useful behaviours into defined 'skills'. Thus courses may vary in either their definition of skills or in their emphases. In our training method we have found that focusing on client feelings and on our own awareness of clients' needs to protect themselves against certain feelings are particularly helpful skills in working with loss. What is important in training is the integration of the relevant skills programme into the overall counselling training, rather than the way in which individual skills are described. A counsellor response which is clear in itself and consonant with the overall counselling framework is one which is most likely to be effective.

HOW TO SELECT A COURSE

From what has been written so far it could be assumed that loss counselling courses are common. Unfortunately they are not. There are still few such specific courses linking loss and counselling, and the majority of those which do exist are arranged under the auspices of Cruse (see Appendix A). Some counselling skills and counsellor training courses avoid looking at loss at all or do not integrate the loss element into the learning. They may, for instance, consider loss in a very academic way (e.g. a series of lectures on 'the stages of grief') without involving the learners as people with their own experiences of grief. The omission of the experiential learning may, of course, be a way of avoiding the pain of loss. This non-experiential approach is, however, of extremely limited effectiveness in improving the ability to relate to the grieving.

Assuming you have found a course which integrates the loss element, then you need to consider the following questions to help you decide which course to choose: What are the entry requirements? To what level do you wish to be trained? How do your aims and objectives match those of the course? How does the course assess the progress of the trainees? How experienced are the trainers? These questions are addressed next.

Entry requirements

It is important to check entry requirements. Some courses in certain institutions require academic qualifications, most do not. Most courses, however, do require applicants to be working in a setting which enables them to practise their counselling skills. If you are unsure how an individual course requirement relates to your own experience (and current activities), check with the course concerned.

Range, level and limitations

Courses in counselling vary from a half-day introductory course to a 3- or 4-year part-time diploma. In general they all fall into one of two very broad categories; introductory or substantial. Introductory courses vary widely in length, between 5 and 100 hours. The shorter ones are usually without restricted entry and often focus on how counselling differs from other forms of helping. On the longer introductory courses, often offering a 'certificate in counselling skills', there may well be a considerable programme of counselling skills. Trainees might, for instance, find themselves practising all the basic skills outlined in chapters 9 and 10. Courses of this nature should also enable participants to explore the implications of using counselling skills in their work and in their personal lives. Many people choose such a course to develop the counselling skills necessary to improve their work in another professional area. Sometimes these skills courses take place within a particular context or around a particular theme, such as 'loss counselling', in which case they might use many of the elements of this book. The BAC Code of Ethics and Practice for Counselling Skills outlines the counselling skills area and defines ethical practice for those using skills in this way.

The longer or 'substantial' training courses, usually 1 year full-time or 2 to 3 years part-time, might be chosen by those wishing eventually to become professional counsellors. Such courses will use all the elements of this book and more. BAC has now created a scheme for the recognition of substantial courses. Guidelines have been developed (BAC Guidelines for the Recognition of Counsellor Training Courses, Appendix C), and a number of organisations offering such counsellor training courses have been recognised in this way. Entry to these and similar courses is through a co-operative selection process where trainees can assess the appropriateness of the course for them and trainers can select the most suitable candidates. Trainers will be looking for people who are open to change and who are no longer too burdened by their own losses.

The Association for Student Counselling (ASC), a division of BAC, produces a 'Guide to Training Courses in Counselling' for BAC, which gives information about a wide range of such 'substantial' courses. Many BAC accredited counsellors (see chapter 15) have taken a 'substantial' course of training. It is not yet (1992) necessary to have been trained on a recognised course in order to become an accredited counsellor. However, those seeking individual accreditation from BAC would be wise to choose a recognised course wherever possible. Needless to say the completion of a recognised course is not enough to gain individual accreditation. There are still the criteria of supervised counselling practice and ongoing personal development to be fulfilled (see BAC Code of Ethics and Practice for Counsellors, Appendix C).

This is a time of rapid change in counselling training, as national standards and qualifications in the field of counselling, counselling skills and interpersonal skills are being developed. It is likely that such developments will lead to a more modular and competency-focused approach to counselling training. This could mean that it would be possible to shape your training in a more rational and consistent way than is sometimes possible at present. Meanwhile, there is a wide range of courses of varying lengths and standards. It should be borne in mind that there is currently little quality control of training, particularly where the shorter courses are concerned. It is important, therefore, to get as much information as you can about any course you are interested in.

It is essential, if you want to work with people at greater depth and help them through the longer-term effects of loss, that you choose a longer course. Courses of different lengths will have different aims and objectives. The following brief outlines give an indication of the aims and limitations of different levels of counselling courses.

A 2-day course such as an 'introduction to the nature of counselling' for lay workers from churches, synagogues or gurdwaras could only have the rather limited aims of helping these workers to learn more about the possible role of counselling in working with bereavement in the community. It could, for instance, offer a definition of what counselling is, and is not; a brief introduction to the attitudes of counselling and to the nature of experiential learning. However, it could only offer very limited self-exploration or practice in the use of counselling skills.

A 1-year in-service course on 'counselling skills' of 2½ hours on one evening a week could offer more. It might, for instance, be arranged for a health centre team of doctors, nurses, health visitors and social workers wishing to improve the quality of patient care in their region, where increasing unemployment means that many people are suffering loss. The course could offer considerable practice in the use of basic counselling skills, some self-exploration and perhaps some discussion on referrals and team functioning. Knowledge of local initiatives, either voluntary or paid, would also be a useful adjunct to such a course. In-depth practice of advanced skills and ongoing supervised counselling practice, however, would not be possible on this length of course.

A 2-year course in 'advanced loss counselling skills' held 1 day per week for those working in education and social services, who have already completed a previous introductory course and are currently working with clients who have suffered loss, would be considerably more detailed. It would be able to offer a greater range and practice of counselling skills. It could also include supervised counselling practice and have a specific focus on work with particular people, such as children or the elderly.

Sometimes a particular group needs specific learning for a special purpose. Then it may be more effective to seek a course tailored to their learning needs. For instance, members of the police and victim support teams may be interested in co-operating to set up a week-long 'intensive skills course' to help them work more effectively with the powerful feelings of loss arising in victims of crime, who are in crisis.

It is evident that counselling training comes in many shapes and sizes. Course providers, regardless of level, have to be clear about how much it is possible for them to achieve.

Aims, objectives and assessment

When selecting a course it is important to consider whether the aims of the course fit with the general direction of your professional development. Course aims will vary from a relatively unfocused aim such as 'to provide an introduction to the nature of counselling', to more specific aims linked to the needs of a target group as illustrated above. It is also important to consider whether the specific course objectives are close enough to your own learning objectives and hence whether the assessment actually monitors the changes you wish to make. If we liken a course to a journey, then this distinction may become clearer. The general aim for a journey might be 'to go south this summer', whereas the specific objectives might be 'first to reach Calais by dawn tomorrow, second to get beyond Paris 3 days later and, finally, to reach the Mediterranean by the end of next week'. On a journey it is easy, with such clear objectives, to assess whether or not the targets at each stage of the journey have been reached. If you have reached Calais by dawn the next day you have passed, but if you are still at sea you still have more work to do. This would be true at each stage of the journey. With counselling courses it is less easy to recognise which target is to be reached at which stage, so it is important to outline as clearly as possible which skills should be acquired, in which order, and to what level.

Consistently demonstrating empathic responses at empathy level 2 (see chapter 9) could be equivalent to 'Calais at dawn' on a substantial training course in counselling skills. A demonstration of clear and effective clarifying might equate with 'Paris 3 days later' and demonstration of a range of more complex skills (e.g. working with protective patterns) together with proof of considerable self-exploration might constitute 'the Mediterranean'. We have given specific times for particular targets on the journey, as this corresponds with the time structures of a course. Most courses also have a system for enabling those who take longer over a particular stage to do the extra work needed to catch up.

The clearer the objectives of a course the easier it is to formulate the criteria for assessment. If one of the course objectives is that 'participants should be able, after thirty sessions of the course, to demonstrate empathic listening towards another course member at level 3' (Exercise 9.4), then it should be possible to assess this at the appropriate stage. This particular skill might be demonstrated with a video-recording of work done with a fellow-trainee as a client, or through an audio-tape of the trainee's counselling practice. Both trainee and trainer would then be in a clearer position to decide whether or not the first target had been reached, and whether the next target was appropriate.

Qualifications of trainers

It is not enough to establish entry requirements, length and level of course, aims and assessment methods. The training and relevant experience of tutors is also important. What are their qualifications? What is their experience of supervised counselling practice?

Tutors should be trained and practising counsellors themselves and at least one should be a BAC accredited counsellor. Following the recent introduction of a scheme for the recognition of trainers by BAC you should also expect at least one of the tutors to have such trainer recognition.

GUIDELINES FOR TRAINERS

Needless to say everything we have said above is as important to prospective trainers as it is to trainees, so in this next section we focus specifically on trainers.

Quality of trainers

Counselling trainers should be trained both in counselling to a level higher than that of the course which they are running, and also in counselling training itself. Further, they should be actively seeking ways of increasing their own professional development and self-awareness. The BAC Code of Ethics and Practice for Trainers seeks to establish and maintain standards for trainers, and to inform and protect members of the public seeking counselling training. Trainers should themselves have some supervised counselling practice as well as consultancy-supervision for their training work.

Counselling trainers are encouraged to work as members of a team. Loss counsellors in particular need also to have worked extensively on the losses in their own lives. This self-knowledge and the team approach are particularly important in the context of self-exploratory work, where there needs to be a safe-enough structure within which trainees can adequately explore their own losses. This 'safe-enough structure' would include using the same comfortable rooms throughout; enough time to explore adequately the feelings raised; a tutorial team who could co-operate in taking care of distressed students and tutors who were not burdened by their own losses.

Publicity material

Publicity material should be clear about the exact time requirements, the place of study, any residential periods, costs, and general level of work and commitment; together with clarity about the nature of the counselling training. This enables the setting up of a clear training contract which then models good practice for those learning about counselling contracts. To enable potential participants to assess what the course requirements are and whether a particular course is suitable for their learning needs, it is also important for trainers to be as clear as possible about all the areas we have outlined in this chapter. Many trainers have found it helpful to address the issues raised in the BAC 'Guide to the Recognition of Courses' even when they are not planning to enter the recognition process.

ENDINGS

We outlined in chapter 10 how important it is to recognise that the endings of both counselling sessions and counselling relationships will often re-awaken old feelings about loss and separations. We saw the importance of structuring endings clearly and firmly so that the ending with the counsellor, at least, can be predictable and the associated feelings can be recognised. These factors are equally true of loss counselling training courses. The ending of the course will, of course, evoke feelings. Training time needs to be allocated, well in advance of the ending, to consider such feelings and to involve trainees in the procedures and rituals created for the ending of the course. Having the experience of being involved in 'creating an ending' can be fun for trainees and will help them grow in confidence in managing endings for themselves. This in turn, helps them to be more confident in enabling their clients to create and contribute to their own endings.

But separations and endings, as we saw with birth, weaning and leaving home, are also beginnings. So, too, the end of a counselling relationship and the end of a training course are also 'beginnings'. The participants will separate, having to trust that the learning they have integrated will help them with the new struggles which, certainly, lie ahead.

We hope that as you end the reading of this book you will have learned or discovered things relevant to you. For us, drawing on our knowledge and experience and having to formulate our ideas in order to write this down has certainly been a learning process! And yet, in the end these ideas are not truly new, only recombined and reformulated for our times.

Shakespeare's timeless formulation, spoken by Malcolm, of MacDuff's need, and indeed right, to express his feelings associated with the loss of his family still seems to us to be the clearest:

Give sorrow words; the grief that does not speak
Whispers the oe'r-fraught heart and bids it break.

Macbeth, Act IV, Scene III

SUMMARY

1 Loss counselling training, like all counselling training, needs to be largely experiential in nature. It should include training in specific skills, knowledge for at least one counselling model, knowledge about loss and the opportunity of self-exploration, both individually and in groups.
2 Supervision (group, individual or both) on a loss-counselling training course enables the integration of skills, knowledge and experience into counselling practice.
3 Some counselling courses offer a specific component on 'loss', others integrate the theory and practice of loss into the whole course.
4 When selecting a course it is important to consider your own learning needs; the length, general aim and target group for the course; the specific objectives and assessments; the balance of self-exploration, knowledge and skills; the availability of supervised counselling practice; and the experience and qualifications of the trainers.
5 Trainers also need to address the issues raised above, as well as to assess their own training skills and levels of supervision. They are also responsible for clear publicity and 'safe enough structures' for personal development work.
6 BAC produces some relevant publications. These are a 'Guide to the Recognition of Training Course', a 'Guide to Training Courses in Counselling' and the Code of Ethics and Practice for Trainers. The BAC Training Group may also be able to offer advice to those setting up training courses.
7 Endings are also Beginnings.

APPENDICES

APPENDIX A USEFUL RESOURCES

Age Concern, Astral House, 126–8 London Rd, London SW16 4ER. Tel: 081-640 5431. Provides services to elderly people in the UK.

Aids: The Terrence Higgins Trust, 52–4 Gray's Inn Road, London WC1X 8JU. Tel: 071-831 0330 (office) and 071-242 1010 (helpline).

Alzheimer's Disease Society, 158–60 Balham High Road, London SW12 9BN. Tel: 081-675 6557.

BACUP (British Association of Cancer United Patients), 121–3 Charterhouse Street, London EC1M 6AA. Tel: 071-608 1661 and 071-608 1038 (Cancer Counselling Service).

British Association for Counselling, 1 Regent Place, Rugby, CV21 2PJ. Tel: 0788 578328.

British Humanist Association, 14 Lambs Conduit Passage, London WC1R 4RH. Tel: 071-430 0908. Helps with ideas for a non-religious funeral or cremation.

Broken Rites, 30 Steavenson Street, Bowburn, Durham, DH6 5BA. Tel: 091-377 0205. This is a self-help group for separated and divorced clergy wives.

Buddhist Hospice Trust, PO Box 51, Herne Bay, CT6 6TP.

Carers' National Association, 29 Chilworth Mews, London W2 3RG. Tel: 071-724 7776. Network for those who need to care for the ill or disabled.

CAB (Citizens' Advice Bureau). There are branches in most large towns. Look in the *Yellow Pages* under 'Social service and welfare organisations'.

Childline, Faraday Buildings, Addle Hill, London EC4. Tel: 071-239 1000 or 0800 1111 (Children's line). Confidential telephone service for abused children.

Compassionate Friends, (Society of), 6 Denmark Street, Bristol BS1 5DQ. Tel: 0272 2927785. Supports and helps those whose child of any age has died of any cause.

Contact a Family, 16 Strutton Ground, London SW1P 2HP. Tel: 071-222

2211 (helpline). Puts families with disabled children in touch with each other.

Cruse, 126 Sheen Road, Richmond, TW9 1UR. Tel: 081-940 4818. Provides a nationwide service of bereavement counselling, advice and information, and social contact for the bereaved.

Families Need Fathers, BM Families, London WC1N 3XX. Tel: 081-886 0970. Organisation committed to continued shared parenting after separation and divorce. Branches in all major conurbations.

Foundation for Black Families, 11 Kingston Square, Salters Hill, London SE19 1DZ. Tel: 081-761 7228.

Gay Bereavement Project, Unitarian Rooms, Hoop Lane, London NW11 8BS. Tel: 081-455 8894/6844. A telephone support for lesbians and gay men bereaved by the death of a partner.

Gingerbread, 35 Wellington Street, London WC2E 7BN. Tel: 071-240 0953. This group supports single parents and their children.

Hospice Information Service, St Christopher's Hospice, 51 Lawrie Park Road, Sydenham, London SE26 6DZ. Tel: 081-778 9252. Provides information on the nature and location of hospices both in the UK and overseas.

Incest Crisis Centre, 34 Grange Street, Newcastle upon Tyne. Tel: 091-261 5317.

Jewish Bereavement Counselling Service, 1 Cyprus Gardens, London N31 1SP. Tel: 071-349 0839. This service is for Greater London only. Other cities have similar services.

MENCAP (Royal Society for Mentally Handicapped Children and Adults), 123 Golden Lane, London EC1Y 0RT. Tel: 071-253 9433.

Miscarriage Association, c/o Clayton Hospital, Northgate, Wakefield WF1 3JS. Tel: 0924 200799.

Mothers Apart from Their Children (MATCH), 64 Delaware Mansions, Delaware Road, London WC1N 3XX.

National Association for the Childless, Birmingham Settlement, 318 Summer Lane, Birmingham B19 3RL. Tel: 021-359 4887 (office) and 021-359 7359 (helpline).

National Association of Bereavement Services, 68 Chalton Street, London NW1 1JR. Tel: 071-388 2153. Help to set up new bereavement services.

National Association for Widows, 54–7 Allison Street, Digbeth, Birmingham B5 5TH. Tel: 021-643 8348. Self-help for the bereaved. Major towns have Widows Advisory Centres.

National Association of Young People's Counselling and Advisory Services (NAYPCAS), 17–23 Albion Street, Leicester LE1 6GD. Tel. 0533–558763.

National Council for One Parent Families, 255 Kentish Town Road, London NW5 2LX. Tel: 071-267 1361.

National Family Conciliation Council, 155 High Street, Dorking, Surrey RH4 1AD. Some cities have their own conciliation councils.

National Foster Care Association, Francis House, Francis Street, London SW1P 1DE. Tel: 071-828 6266.

National Organisation for Counselling Adoptees and Their Parents (NOR-CAP), 3 New High Street, Headington, Oxford OX3 5AJ. Tel: 0865 750554.

Natural Parents' Support Group, c/o Mary Woolliscroft, 90 Harvey Place, Uttoxeter, Staffs. Support group for women who have given up children for adoption.

Parent Network, 44-6 Caversham Road, London NW5 2DS. Tel: 071-485 8535. Run courses for parents wanting to share problems and improve relationships with children.

Post Adoption Centre, Interchange Building, 15 Wilkin Street, London NW5 3NG. Tel: 071-284 0555. Support organisation for adoptive parents, adopted people and natural parents.

Post-natal Illness, (Association for), c/o 7 Gowan Avenue, London SW6. Tel: 071-831 8996. Support group.

Rape Crisis Centre, PO Box 69, London WC1X 9NJ. Tel: 071-278 3956 (office) and 071-837 1600 (helpline). Most cities have a local rape crisis group.

Relate (Marriage Guidance Association), Herbert Gray College, Little Church Street, Rugby CV21 3AP. Tel: 0788 573241. There are local branches in all towns. Counsellors also work with separating couples and individuals.

SAFTA (Support After Termination for Abnormality), 29-30 Soho Square, London W1V 6JB. Tel: 071-439 6124.

Samaritans, 10 The Grove, Slough, SL1 1QP (Head Office). Have branches in all major cities and towns. For local telephone number look in your local telephone directory under 'S' or emergency. Offers emotional support to anyone in need.

SANDS (Stillbirth and Perinatal Death Association), 15a Christchurch Hill, London NW3 1JY. Tel: 071-833 2851.

SIDS (Foundation for the Study of Infant Death), 35 Belgrave Square, London SW1X 8QB. Tel: 071-235 0965. This organisation offers a Cot Death Helpline 071-235 1721.

Stepfamily (National Association), 72 Willesden Lane, London NW6 7TA. Tel: 071-372 0846. Offers help, advice and support to step-families through publications and a telephone counselling service. Publish a magazine for young people in step-families called 'Stepladder'.

WPF (Westminster Pastoral Foundation), 23 Kensington Square, London W8 5HN. Tel: 071-937 6956. This organisation offers counselling in London and now has branches in other towns.

APPENDIX B FURTHER READING

We have listed here books or chapters of books which we think are useful background reading to each chapter. We have also added novels and biographical material which are a 'good read' and which we have found illuminating. Books that grievers have found particularly useful we have marked with an asterisk (*).

Chapter 1

Bowlby, J. (1979) Lecture 7 in *The Making and Breaking of Affectional Bonds*, London: Tavistock Publications.

Parkes, C.M. and Stevenson-Hinde (1982) Part 1 in *The Place of Attachment in Human Behaviour*, London: Tavistock Publications.

Skynner, R. and Cleese, J. (1984) Especially pages 71–84, 109–30 and 145–64 in *Families and How to Survive Them*, London: Methuen.

Viorst, J. Part 1 in *Necessary Losses*, London: Positive Paperbacks.

Chapter 2

Rogers, C.R. (1967) Especially Parts I and II in *On Becoming a Person*, London: Constable.

Chapter 3

Books about death and bereavement

Kübler-Ross, E. (1970) *On Death and Dying*, London: Tavistock Publications.

Parkes, C.M. (1975) *Bereavement: Studies of Grief in Adult Life*, London: Penguin.

Novels, biographies, anthologies and self-help books which have helped us and other grievers understand more about our experiences of death and dying

*Banks, L.R. (1972) *The Backward Shadow*, London: Penguin.

*Blaiklock, E.M. (1980) *Kathleen. A Record of a Sorrow*, London: Hodder and Stoughton.

*Brown, S. (1984) *Drawing Near to the City*, London: Triangle.

*Collick, E.M. (1986) *Through Grief*, London: Darton, Longman & Todd.

*Craig, M. (1979) *Blessings*, London: Hodder and Stoughton.

*Craven, M. (1967) *I Heard the Owl Call My Name*, London: Picador.

*Hill, S. (1977) *In the Springtime of the Year*, London: Penguin.

*Humphry, D. with Wickett, A. (1978) *Jean's Way*, London: Fontana/ Collins.

*Johnston, J. (1989) *The Christmas Tree*, London: Penguin.

*Kohner, N. and Henley, A. (1991) *When a Baby Dies*, London: Pandora.

*Kushner, H. (1981) *When Bad Things Happen to Good People*, London: Pan.

*Leach, C. (1981) *Letter to a Younger Son*, London: J.M. Dent.

*Lewis, C.S. (1961) *A Grief Observed*, London: Faber.

*Lively, P. (1985) *Perfect Happiness*, London: Penguin.

*—— (1990) *Passing On*, London: Penguin.

*Neustatter, A. with Newson, G. (1986) *Mixed Feelings: Experience of Abortion*, London: Pluto.

*Rollin, B. (1987) *Last Wish*, London: Penguin.

*Tatelbaum, J. (1981) *The Courage to Grieve*, London: Heinemann.

*Taylor, L.M. (1983) *Living with Loss*, London: Fontana.

*Wallbank, S. (1991) *Facing Grief: Bereavement and the Young Adult*, Cambridge: Lutterworth Press.

*Whitacker, A. (ed.) (1984) *All the End is Harvest*, London: Darton, Longman & Todd.

*Zorza, R. and Zorza, V. (1980) *A Way to Die*, London: Sphere.

Chapter 4

Bowlby, J. (1980) *Attachment and Loss: Volume 3: Loss: Sadness and Depression*, London: Penguin.

Hinton, J. (1967) *Dying*, London: Penguin.

Parkes, C.M. (1975) *Bereavement: Studies of Grief in Adult Life*, London: Penguin.

Raphael, B. (1984) *The Anatomy of Bereavement*, London: Unwin Hyman.

Worden, J.W. (1983) *Grief Counselling and Grief Therapy*, London: Tavistock.

Chapter 5

Aries, P. (1974) *Western Attitudes towards Death: from the Middle Ages to the Present*, Baltimore, Md.: Johns Hopkins University Press.

Elias, N. (1985) *The Loneliness of the Dying*, Oxford: Blackwell.

Gorer, G. (1965) *Death, Grief and Mourning in Contemporary Britain*, London: Cresset.

Hockey, J. (1990) *Experiences of Death*, Edinburgh: Edinburgh University Press.

Chapter 6

Ainsworth-Smith, I. and Speck, P. (1982) *Letting Go: Caring for the Dying and Bereaved*, London: SPCK.

D'Ardenne, P. and Mahtani, A. (1989) *Transcultural Counselling in Action*, London: Sage.

Feild, R. (1979) *The Invisible Way: a Time to Love and a Time to Die*, Dorset: Element Books.

Gibran, K. (1991) *The Prophet*, London: Pan.

Huntingdon, R. and Metcalfe, P. (1979) *Celebrations of Death*, Cambridge: Cambridge University Press.

Kübler-Ross, E. (1986) *Death: the Final Stage of Growth*, New Jersey: Prentice-Hall.

Lago, C. and Thompson, J. (1989) 'Counselling and race', in W. Dryden, D. Charles-Edwards and R. Woolfe (eds) *Handbook of Counselling in Britain*, London: Routledge.

Neuberger, J. (1987) *Caring for Dying People of Different Faiths*, London: Austen Cornish for Lisa Sainsbury Foundation.

Chapter 7

Anthony, S. (1971) *The Discovery of Death in Childhood and After*, London: Allen Lane.

Bluebond-Langer, M. (1978) *The Private World of Dying Children*, New Jersey: Princeton University Press.

Fabian, A. (1988) *The Daniel Diary*, London: Grafton.

Fraiberg, S.H. (1959) *The Magic Years*, London: Methuen.

Furman, E. (1974) *A Child's Parent Dies*, New Haven, Conn.: Yale University Press.

Krementz, J. (1983) *How it Feels when a Parent Dies*, London: Gollancz.

Noonan, E. (1983) *Counselling Young People*, London: Methuen.

Chapter 8

Bowlby, J. (1979) Lecture 5 in *The Making and Breaking of Affectional Bonds*, London: Tavistock Publications.

Burgoyne, J. (1984) *Breaking Even: Divorce, Your Children and You*, London: Penguin.

Clulow, C. and Mattinson, J. (1989) *Marriage Inside Out*, London: Penguin.

Pincus, L. (1976) *Death and the Family*, London: Faber.

Pincus, L. and Dare, C. (1978) *Secrets in the Family*, London: Faber.

Skynner, R. and Cleese, J. (1984) Especially pages 15–42 in *Families and How to Survive Them*, London: Methuen.

Chapters 9 and 10

Jacobs, M. (1988) *Psychodynamic Counselling in Action*, London: Sage.

Mearns, D. and Thorne, B. (1988) *Person-Centred Counselling in Action*, London: Sage.

Munro, E.E., Manthei, R.J. and Small, J.J. (1983) *Counselling: a Skills Approach*, New Zealand: Methuen.

Nelson-Jones, R. (1983) *Practical Counselling Skills*, London: Holt, Rinehart and Winston.

Chapter 11

Books about how to work with children

Jewett, C. (1984) *Helping Children Cope with Separation and Loss*, London: Batsford Ltd.

Wells, R. (1983) *Helping Children Cope with Grief*, London: Tavistock Publications.

Books which children have found helpful

We have given a rough indication of the appropriate age-group, knowing that children go back and forwards in their reading ages.

3–7 years old

Althea (1980) *I Have Two Homes*, Cambridge: Dinosaur.

—— (1982) *When Uncle Bob Died*, Cambridge: Dinosaur.

Burningham, J. (1984) *Granpa*, London: Jonathan Cape.

Heegaard, M.E. (1988) *When Someone Very Special Dies*, Minneapolis: Woodland Press.

Selby, J. (1975) *The Day Granma Died*, London: Church Information Office

Stickney, D. (1984) *Water Bugs and Dragonflies*, London: Mowbray.

Varley, S. (1985) *Badger's Parting Gifts*, London: Collins Picture Lions.

Viorst, J. (1972) *The Tenth Good Thing About Barney*, London: Collins

A number of traditional fairy tales also explore loss and separation, e.g. *The Babes in the Wood, Snow White and the Seven Dwarfs, Rumpelstiltskin.*

8–13 years old

Alexander, S. (1988) *Leila*, London: Hamish Hamilton.

Anderson, R. (1984) *The Poacher's Son*, London: Fontana Lions.

Ashley, B. (1981) *Dodgem*, London: Penguin.

Little, J. (1984) *Mama's Going to Buy You a Mockingbird*, London: Penguin.

Magorian, M. (1983) *Good Night Mr Tom*, London: Penguin.

Marshall, J.V. (1980) *Walkabout*, London: Penguin.

Patterson, K. (1980) *Bridge to Tarabitha*, London: Penguin.

Paton-Walsh, J. (1987) *Gaffer Samson's Luck*, London: Penguin.

Saint-Exupéry, A. (1974) *The Little Prince*, London: Piccolo.

Townsend, S. (1983) *The Secret Diary of Adrian Mole Aged 13 3/4*, London: Methuen.
White, E.B. (1952) *Charlotte's Web*, London: Penguin.

13 years upwards

Branfield, J. (1981) *Fox in Winter*, London: Collins.
Blume, J. (1983) *Tiger Eyes*, London: Piccolo.
Dickens, C. (1978) *Nicholas Nickleby*, London: Penguin.
—— (1978) *Oliver Twist*, London: Penguin.
Guy, R. (1989) *The Friends*, London: Penguin.
Howker, J. (1984) *Badger on the Barge and Other Stories*, London: Armada.
—— (1987) *Isaac Campion*, London: Armada.
Hoy, L. (1984) *Your Friend Rebecca*, London: Collins.
Hunter, M. (1988) *A Sound of Chariots*, London: Armada.
Oneal, Z. (1985) *A Formal Feeling*, London: Armada.
Serrailer, I. (1960) *The Silver Sword*, London: Puffin.
Williams, G. and Ross, J. (1983) *When People Die*, London: MacDonald.
Zindel, P. (1982) *The Pigman's Legacy*, London: Penguin.

Chapter 12

Bowlby, J. (1980) Lectures 1 and 2 in *The Making and Breaking of Affectional Bonds*, London: Tavistock Publications.
Rowe, D. (1983) *Depression: The Way Out of Your Prison*, London: Routledge.
Skynner, R. and Cleese, J. (1984) Parts of chapters 1 and 4 in *Families and How to Survive Them*, London: Methuen.
Viorst, J. (1989) Chapters 3, 5, 9 and 16 in *Necessary Losses*, London: Positive Paperbacks.
Winnicott, D.W. (1984) Part II in *Deprivation and Delinquency*, London: Tavistock Publications.

Chapter 13

Jacobs, M. (1988) *Psychodynamic Counselling in Action*, London: Sage.
Kennedy, E. (1977) *On Becoming a Counsellor*, Dublin: Gill and Macmillan.
Lendrum, S. and Syme, G. *Loss Counselling in Practice. An Interactive Video*. Available from Whiting and Birch, 90 Dartmouth Rd, Forest Hill, London SE23 3HZ.
Useful for counsellors, and for clients abused as children:
Bass, E. and Davies, L. (1990) *The Courage to Heal*, London: Cedar.
Gil, E. (1983) *Outgrowing the Pain*, New York: Dell Publishing.

Chapter 14

Jacobs, M. (1988) Chapter 3 in *Psychodynamic Counselling in Action*, London: Sage.

Kennedy, E. (1977) Chapter 16 in *On Becoming a Counsellor*, Dublin: Gill and Macmillan.

Chapter 15

Dryden, W. and Thorne, B. (1991) *Training and Supervision for Counselling in Action*, London: Sage.

Hawkins, P. and Shohet, R. (1989) *Supervision in the Helping Professions*, Milton Keynes: Open University Press.

Mearns, D. and Dryden, W. (1990) *Experiences of Counselling in Action*, London: Sage.

Proctor, B. (1988) *Supervision, a Working Alliance (Videotape training manual)*, St Leonards-on-Sea, E. Sussex: Alexia Publications.

Chapter 16

Dryden, W. and Thorne, B. (1991) *Training and Supervision for Counselling in Action*, London: Sage.

Hobson, R.F. and Margison, F. (1982) *A Converstaional Model of Psychotherapy* (3 training videotapes), University of Manchester.

The following manuals are useful for trainers.

Inskipp, F. (1985) *A Manual for Trainers*, Cambridge: National Extension College.

Machin, L. (1991) *Looking at Loss*, London: Longman.

Ward, B. and Houghton, J. (1988) *Good Grief*, London: Cruse.

Warman, J. and Fisher, M. (1991) *Bereavement and Loss*, Cambridge: National Extension College.

Woolfe, R. (1990) *Counselling Skills: a Training Manual*, Edinburgh: Scottish Health Education Council.

APPENDIX C LIST OF USEFUL BAC PUBLICATIONS

Basic Principles of Counselling
Code of Ethics and Practice for Counselling Skills
Code of Ethics and Practice for Counsellors
Code of Ethics and Practice for Supervisors
Code of Ethics and Practice for Trainers
Counselling and Psychotherapy Resources Directory
Directory of Trainers
Directory of Training Courses in Counselling and Psychotherapy

Guide for Recognition of Courses
Guide to Training Courses

Handbook of Counselling in Britain (1989) Edited by W. Dryden, D. Charles-Edwards and R. Woolfe. Published by Routledge in association with BAC.

HIV Counselling; Report on National Survey and Consultation, 1990. BAC/Dept of Health Joint Project.

REFERENCES

Ainsworth, M.D.S., Blehar, M.C., Waters, E. and Wall, S. (1978) *Patterns of Attachment: a psychological study of the strange situation*, Hillsdale, NJ: Lawrence Erlbaum Associates.

Bowlby, J. (1969) *Attachment and Loss: Volume 1: Attachment*, London: Penguin Books.

—— (1979) *The Making and Breaking of Affectional Bonds*, London: Tavistock Publications.

—— (1980) *Attachment and Loss: Volume 3: Loss: Sadness and Depression*, London: Penguin Books.

Brown, G.W. and Harris, T. (1978) *Social Origins of Depression*, London: Tavistock Publications.

Burgoyne, J. (1984) *Breaking Even: Divorce, Your Children and You*, London: Penguin Books.

Clulow, C. and Mattinson, J. (1989) *Marriage Inside Out*, London: Penguin Books.

Firth, R. (1961) *Elements of Social Organisation*, London: Tavistock Publications.

Franchino, L. (1987) *Basic Counselling Skills*, London: Cruse.

Fromm, E. (1978) *To Have or To Be*, London: Jonathan Cape.

Harlow, H.F. (1961) 'The development of affectional patterns in infant monkeys', in B.M. Foss (ed.) *Determinants of Infant Behaviour: Volume l*, London: Methuen.

Heegaard, M.E. (1988) *When Someone Very Special Dies*, Minneapolis: Woodland Press.

Hockey, J. (1990) *Experiences of Death: an Anthropological Account*, Edinburgh: Edinburgh University Press.

Jewett, C. (1984) *Helping Children Cope with Separation and Loss*, London: B. T. Batsford Ltd.

Malinowski, B. (1925) 'Magic, science and religion', in J. Needham (ed.) *Science, Religion and Reality*, London: The Sheldon Press.

Mearns, D. and Thorne, B. (1988) *Person-Centred Counselling in Action*, London: Sage Publications.

Miller, A. (1983) *The Drama of the Gifted Child*, London: Faber and Faber.

Mørch, D.T. (1982) *The Evening Star*, London: Serpent's Tail.

Parkes, C.M. (1972) *Bereavement: Studies of Grief in Adult Life*, London: Tavistock Publications.

Proctor, B. (1988) *Supervision: a Working Alliance* (Videotape training manual), St Leonards-on-Sea, E. Sussex: Alexia Publications.

Raphael, B. (1984) *The Anatomy of Bereavement*, London: Unwin Hyman.

Rochlin, G. (1967) 'How younger children view death and themselves', in E.A. Grollman (ed.) *Explaining Death to Children*, Boston: Beacon Press.

REFERENCES

Rogers, C.R. (1967) *On Becoming a Person*, London: Constable.

Searles, H. F. (1955) *The Informational Value of the Supervisor's Emotional Experience. Collected Papers on Schizophrenia and Related Subjects*, London: Hogarth.

Spitz, R. (1945) *Hospitalism. The Psychoanalytic Study of the Child. Volume 1*, New York: International Universities Press, Inc.

Stern, D. (1985) *The Interpersonal World of the Infant*, New York: Basic Books.

Suttie, I.D. (1935) *The Origins of Love and Hate*, London: Kegan Paul.

Thorne, B. and Dryden, W. (1991) 'Key issues in the training of counsellors', in W. Dryden and B. Thorne (eds) *Training and Supervision for Counselling in Action*, London: Sage.

Truax, C.B. and Carkhuff, R.R. (1967) *Towards Effective Counseling and Psychotherapy: Training and Practice*, Chicago: Aldine Publishing Co.

Van Eerdewegh, M.M., Bieri, M.D., Parilla, R.H. and Clayton, P.J. (1982) 'The bereaved child', *British Journal of Psychiatry* 140: 23–9.

Viorst, J. (1989) *Necessary Losses*, London: Positive Paperbacks.

Winnicott, D.W. (1949) 'Hate in the counter-transference', *International Journal of Psycho-Analysis* 30: 69–75.

—— (1964) *The Child, The Family, and the Outside World*, London: Penguin Books.

Worden, J.W. (1983) *Grief Counselling and Grief Therapy*, London: Tavistock Publications.

NAME INDEX

Ainsworth, M.D.S. 7, 8, 12, 37

Bowlby, J. 6, 7, 11, 22, 37, 45, 47, 48, 59, 112, 167
Brown, G.W. 58
Burgoyne. J. 63

Carkhuff, R.R. 16, 82, 181
Clulow, C. 63

Darwin, C. 22
Dryden, W. 179

Firth, R. 47
Freud, S. 6, 43
Fromm, E. 56

Harlow, H.F. 7
Harris, T. 58
Heegaard, M. 116
Hinton, J. 45
Hockey, J. 44, 45

Jewett, C. 116, 119

Kübler-Ross, E. 45

Lorenz, K. 6

Malinowski, B. 47
Mattinson, J. 63
Mearns, D. 82, 93

Mørch, D.T. 16

Parkes, C.M. 22, 31, 32, 33, 37, 38, 45, 76, 77
Proctor, B. 166

Raphael, B. 30, 45, 66
Robertson, James 10, 12
Robertson, Joyce 10, 12
Rochlin, G. 59
Rogers, C.R. 17

Saunders, C. 45
Searles, H.F. 173
Shakespeare, W. 6, 186, 187
Spitz, R. 7
Stern, D. 3
Suttie, I.D. 7
Swinburne, A.C. vi, xii

Thorne, B. 82, 93, 179
Tinbergen, N. 6
Truax, C.B. 16, 82, 181

Van Eerdewegh, M.M. 65
Viorst, J. 3

Winnicott, D.W. 126, 127
Worden, W. 33

Zorza, R. 45
Zorza, V. 45

SUBJECT INDEX